Quick and easy

handmade cards

Quick and easy

handmade cards

Petra Boase

hamlyn

First published in Great Britain in 2005 by
Hamlyn, a division of Octopus Publishing Group Ltd
2–4 Heron Quays, London E14 4JP

Distributed in the United States and Canada by
Sterling Publishing Co., Inc.
387 Park Avenue South, New York, NY 10016-8810

ISBN-13: 978-0-600-61243-8
ISBN-10: 0-600-61243-0

A CIP catalogue record for this book is available
from the British Library

Printed and bound in China

10 9 8 7 6 5 4 3

Note
While the advice and information in this book is
believed to be accurate, neither the author nor the
publisher will be responsible for any injury, losses,
damages, actions, proceedings, claims, demands,
expenses and costs (including legal costs or
expenses) incurred or in any way arising out of
following the projects in this book.

Contents

Introduction

Despite living in a fast-moving age of computer and mobile phone communication, there is still nothing more heart-warming than receiving a handmade greeting card, lovingly crafted by the sender. Making your own cards is hugely rewarding – not only is it a form of relaxation but it provides an outlet for your creativity and the end result is bound to be appreciated and treasured above any shop-bought card.

There are many occasions when a special, handmade card would be appreciated. The book is divided into four sections covering the most popular topics: Festive fun – dates such as Christmas and Easter, when it is traditional to send a card to mark the festivities; Celebrations – cards for those special moments such as a wedding or birth of a new baby; Birthday – a selection of cards that can be adapted to suit any birthday girl or boy; and Everyday greetings – for when you just want to say hello or thank you. Handmade cards are the perfect choice for party invitations too, as you can personalize them with all the necessary details. Any of the cards in the book could be used in this way, but for invitations and thank-you notes you often need multiple copies – see Good luck horseshoe (see page 62), Bon voyage (see page 94) and Embossed tin love heart (see page 58), for some ideas.

The projects throughout the book are designed to kick start your imagination and show you a variety of simple card-making styles and techniques. Straightforward collage, appliqué, needlepoint, rubber stamping, papercrafting to create 3-D effects, wire work, and decoupage – all techniques that can be easily achieved around the kitchen table in just a couple of hours.

All the basic techniques that are used in the projects are explained in the Tips and techniques section (see pages 12–14), with easy-to-follow photographs showing you how to transfer templates, cut out shapes and stencils, and finish your cards, including making and decorating envelopes. There is also a section on which tools you will need and how to use them (see pages 8–9), plus an overview of the materials and tools that are required (see pages 10–11).

Art and craft stores are an Aladdin's cave of papers, tools and embellishments, and you can end up spending much more than you need. A list of equipment is provided to help get you started and soon you will find that a stock of paper, card, glue and a few decorations will provide the starting point for many imaginative ideas.

Ready-made card blanks, stickers, stamps and pre-cut shapes are all available but by looking closer to home you will produce individual cards that have your own personal touch, at half the price. Be creative and look around for everyday items, such as old scraps of fabric, paper, even wallpaper, with which to decorate your cards. Old photographs, magazine cuttings, pressed flowers – all can be used to give your card an individual twist. Many of the projects use scraps of fabric and ribbon to great effect – see Baby patchwork (see page 48), Polka dot present (see page 78), Embroidered cupcake (see page 74) and Button flower (see page 102) for some ideas. Drawing an original design or pattern can be a stumbling block and that is why the templates of all the motifs on the cards are provided at actual size, so that you can get started straight away. Each section in the book concludes with a gallery of cards by other card makers, to inspire you further.

All the cards can be personalized in different ways to make them unique to you – choose an alternative colour theme, or a different-sized card, adapt the pattern or shapes and mix and match templates or motifs. Simplicity is the key, and if you bear in mind that 'less is more', you will produce stylish, individual cards to be proud of.

Good luck!

tools

The great thing about paper craft is that you don't need to invest in lots of expensive, technical equipment. For general card making a craft knife, cutting mat, ruler, pair of scissors and pot of PVA glue will be sufficient to get you started. There are some techniques that require more specialist equipment, such as jewellery pliers or lino cutters, and it is worth investing in these as and when required.

Cutting out

Invest in a good pair of general scissors, together with a smaller pair for cutting fabric and threads. Never use your fabric scissors for cutting card as this will blunt them. For cutting windows or intricate patterns a craft knife and cutting mat are essential.

Craft knife (scalpel) This is an invaluable tool when making greeting cards. Choose a knife where you can replace the blades or snap them off to ensure that your blade is always sharp, this is important for clean cutting lines. Rotary cutters are good for card and fabric. Use with a cutting mat to protect your work surface from cuts and scratches, and with a metal edge ruler to ensure a straight line and safe cutting.

Craft scissors These are good all round scissors for cutting paper, card and other craft materials.

Cutting mat A rubberized, self-healing mat to be used when cutting paper, card or fabric with a craft knife to protect work surfaces. Mats are available in different sizes (from A1 to A5) and many feature a useful grid for keeping your angles square.

Embroidery scissors Small sharp scissors used for finer sewing projects and cutting threads.

Fabric scissors Sharp scissors used for cutting fabric, do not use for cutting paper or card as they will soon become blunt.

Lino cutter and blades Use for cutting in to lino to make a print block. Different size blades are fixed into the handle one at a time to create different cuts in the lino, such as a fine blade for cutting intricate details.

Paper punch Patterned paper punches are available in a range of shapes and can be used on paper and card. Border and corner punches are also available. A simple hole punch can also be used for creating perfect dots.

Patterned scissors Scissors with patterned blades are readily available which give you the option of cutting fabric or card with a patterned edge, such as scalloped, wavy, deckle and the classic pinking shears for a zigzag effect.

General tools

Keep a pencil, ruler and eraser to hand in your craft box alongside your cutting equipment as they are all invaluable for marking and measuring cards, templates and decorations.

Embossing tool and mat Similar to a pen, this tool has a rounded end that is used for embossing shapes on special

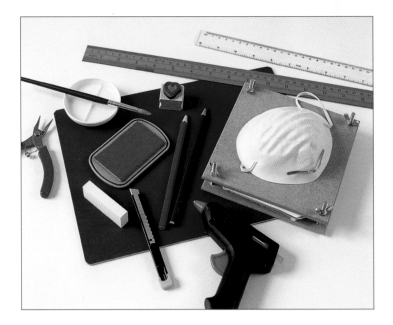

Sticking equipment

Many brands of PVA glue are available with an integral brush or a nozzle for accurate application but you will find a separate brush useful for applying large areas of glue, and for following a shape or stencil.

Glue brush A basic painting brush to apply PVA water-based glue. Wash after each use.

Glue gun A very useful tool for when you want glue to dry quickly, or for sticking small items. Hot glue guns should be handled with care.

Paper

Paper and card are the basic ingredients for any card making project. Available in a rainbow of colours and tones, plain or patterned, textured or metallic, thick or thin, the choice is endless. In addition to this huge choice is the range of handmade papers, with different colours and textures, some with additions such as petals or leaves. You can also make your own paper.

Paper sizes vary but there are standard sheet sizes available such as A4 (290 x 297 mm/8¼ x 11¹⁄₁₆ in) and A5 (148 x 210 mm /5¹³⁄₁₆ x 8¼ in), which have been used for the projects. Larger sheets of some papers can be purchased and cut down as required. When choosing paper or card, select a thickness or weight that will fold easily and remain rigid (such as 230–260 gsm). The weight of paper is measured in grams per square metre (gsm).

Acetate An opaque, thin sheet of plastic that can be drawn or photocopied onto.

Drawing paper Use a thin, plain white paper for copying templates and patterns.

Card Many of the projects use standard A4 or A5 sheets of card for the folded card blank.

Lino board Used for cutting into to make the base for a lino print.

Thick card Useful for making stencils.

Thin card This is ideal for making templates which need to be flexible but rigid enough to stay in place when drawing around the edges.

Tissue paper Available in a range of colours, this is ideal for adding delicate details or layering, or mounted behind a window or cut-out for a stained glass effect.

Tracing paper Useful for copying and transferring templates.

Translucent paper Parchment or vellum paper has an opaque quality and is available in many colours and patterns. It can be used for embossing or decoration.

Wallpaper Leftover rolls of old wallpaper, especially those with a clear pattern, make a great starting place for collage cards.

parchment paper or metal foil. It is also useful for scoring the crease of greeting cards before folding them in half. Use with a soft embossing mat.

Eraser This is useful for erasing any pencil lines you have used. A smooth-edge eraser can also be used to make a rubber stamp, choose one that is large enough to take your chosen design and can be handled easily.

Face mask This should be worn when using spray adhesive or spray paint to protect you from inhaling the fumes.

Metal edge ruler Use with a craft knife or scalpel to ensure that you cut a straight line and prevent the blade from slipping.

Pencil A sharp pencil is useful for marking measurements or positions, use a soft pencil, such as a 2B, if you need to erase the mark. Use a harder HB pencil for tracing outlines and drawing around templates.

Ruler A long, clear ruler is essential for measuring pieces of paper and finding the centre of the card before folding.

Tweezers These are useful for picking up and placing small sequins or beads, and for applying gold leaf.

Specialist tools

These tools are not essential basic equipment but are worth investing in if you wish to expand your range of techniques.

Flower press Place fresh flowers and leaves between the layers of paper and card and do up tightly.

Jewellery pliers These pliers have a smaller point than normal tools and are easier to use in craft projects.

Rubber covered roller (brayer) Use when making lino prints for spreading ink on the glass surface and applying ink to the lino cut before making a print.

materials

After paper and card, the other materials that you require for handmade cards will very much depend on the style and techniques of the project. For most cards you will need a reliable form of adhesive, be it PVA glue, adhesive tape, spray adhesive or sticky foam pads. Your other materials – from fabric scraps and buttons to craft wire and ink pads – can be acquired separately for each project.

Adhesives

Art and craft stores stock an amazing array of different adhesives but with a pot of PVA glue, a can of spray adhesive and some sticky tape you will be able to assemble most handmade cards.

Adhesive foam pads These are double-sided sticky pads, available in different sizes, that are very useful when you want part of your design to be raised slightly from the background.

Adhesive tape A general tape is useful for sticking backgrounds or securing shapes that will be hidden from view.

Double-sided adhesive tape This tape comes in different widths and is invaluable for sticking down paper or card cut-outs, frames, background panels and collage pieces. Simply peel off the backing paper and smooth down in place. Note: It cannot be repositioned.

Heat adhesive webbing An iron-on webbing used in simple appliqué projects to help stick fabric shapes in place on a background fabric before sewing in position.

PVA glue A versatile, water based, slow-drying adhesive. It sticks paper, card, fabric, buttons, and sequins.

Spray adhesive Available in a spray can that produces a fine spray of adhesive that covers the whole surface with an even layer. It is a quick way of sticking paper and fabric shapes in place and allows for a little repositioning. Cover your surface with newspaper before applying the spray. Note: Spray adhesive is highly-flammable and toxic. Always use in a well-ventilated area and avoid contact with skin and eyes. Wear a face mask and avoid inhaling the vapour.

Decorations

From tiny beads to embossed rubber stamps, your choice of decoration is almost endless.

Beads and buttons Available from haberdashers and craft stores, these make very versatile decorations, from tiny beads to character buttons, all in different shapes, sizes and colours.

Craft wire This comes in different widths (gauges) and colour finishes. Use with a pair of jewellery pliers to bend the wire into different shapes.

Embossing metal A soft craft metal that is easy to cut with scissors or a craft knife. You can impress a pattern onto the metal using an old ballpoint pen or special embossing tool.

Embossing powder This fine powder is available in many colours and needs to be used in conjunction with a binder, such as ink from a rubber stamp. Stamp a shape on the card and sprinkle on the powder, shake off the excess and hold over a heat source until the powder melts to form the shape. Crafter's heat guns are available.

Glitter Available in a wide range of colours and sizes from heavy to fine.

Gold leaf A very thin sheet of gold leaf that can be applied to an adhesive background with a brush.

Sequins Available in standard, plain sizes but also in flower and novelty shapes to suit different occasions.

Pens, paints and inks

A selection of coloured pencils or paints is always good to have close at hand for adding finishing touches.

Coloured pencils These are ideal for adding small, hand-drawn details on cards or for filling in colours on rubber stamp designs.

Fabric marker pen This is useful when drawing around templates onto fabric.

Gutta This is a liquid resist used in silk painting to outline the design. Once dry it acts as a barrier to the silk paint to prevent the colour bleeding outside the edges of the design.

Dye stamping ink Dye inks produce the most vibrant colours and work on all sorts of papers and even fabrics. You can buy refills when your ink pad runs dry.

Pigment stamping ink A slower drying ink that resembles paint. Use on mat, porous paper.

Lino printing ink Available in water or oil based. The water based is quick to dry and easy to clean.

Silk paints These come in many vibrant colours and can be mixed to create more tones. Apply with a fine paintbrush.

Fabrics

Scrap pieces of fabric, felts and wools look very effective on a handmade card. With the addition of ribbon, lace and some simple stitching you can really make the most of all those odds and ends at the bottom of your sewing basket.

Patterns and plains A cotton or cotton/polyester mix fabric is best for cutting out without the risk of the edges fraying. Dress fabric, upholstery fabric and craft fabrics are all suitable. Fabrics with a large pattern are ideal for cutting round for appliqué shapes.

Felt This is easy to cut and shape and is available in a range of colours. For a thicker, more handmade effect, wash the felt in a washing machine: some shrinkage may occur.

Lace This is very effective on its own or used as a stencil to recreate the pattern in ink or paint.

Ribbons There are many textures, colours and patterns available which will enhance any card design.

Silk A shiny surface that is not easy to cut into specific shapes but makes a good background for painting in conjunction with a gutta resist liquid.

Threads Cotton, wool and silk threads are useful for adding stitched decorations or finishing appliqué pieces.

Wool Similar to felt but more delicate, wool gives a very soft effect perfect for baby cards.

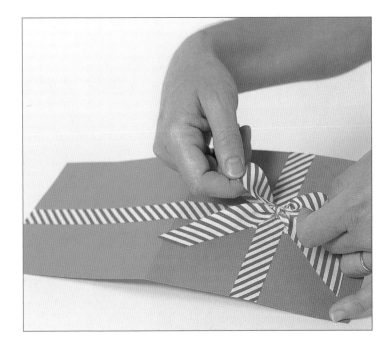

tips and techniques

These basic techniques will help you to transfer motifs onto card to make templates or stencils, show you how to create a card blank with a neat crease and explain simple appliqué stitches. There are also tips on making and decorating envelopes to finish your cards with style.

Making a template

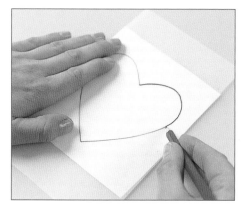

1 Draw over the outlines of the template on a sheet of tracing paper with a soft pencil.

2 Turn the tracing paper over and scribble pencil marks on the reverse over the traced image.

3 Place the tracing paper scribbled side down on a piece of thin card and draw over the outlines again to transfer the design.

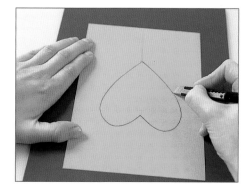

4 Remove the tracing paper to reveal the shape and cut out the template using scissors or a craft knife.

Making a stencil

1 Trace and transfer the design as described in 'Making a template' (see left), onto thick card or plastic.

2 Using a craft knife and cutting mat, carefully cut around the edges of the design and remove the card to reveal the shape.

3 To use the stencil, place over your card and fix in place either with spray adhesive or masking tape. You can apply paint, glue or spray paint to the stencil.

4 When the paint or glue is tacky, carefully remove the stencil to reveal the design.

Folding a card

1 Cut out the piece of card to the required size. Use a ruler to divide the card in half and mark the centre points with an embossing tool. Alternatively, line up the centre with a gridline on your cutting mat.

2 With the embossing tool and a ruler, draw a line joining the embossed marks and fold the card in half. If you don't have an embossing tool, the back of a table knife or a bone folder will also score the card. For a neat crease, run a metal spoon along the edge.

Making a zigzag fold

1 Divide the height of the paper by three and mark out the third divisions using an embossing tool.

2 Score and fold the first line using the embossing tool against a ruler. Fold the crease back.

3 Turn the card over and score the second line with the embossing tool and ruler and fold the crease back. The two folds should go in opposite directions.

Applying gold leaf (see Golden reindeer, page 24)

1 Either use a stencil to apply a PVA glue shape to the card, or apply random spots of glue.

2 When the glue is tacky, remove the stencil and apply the gold leaf carefully, holding one edge with tweezers while you smooth down the gold leaf with a brush.

3 Gently brush away the excess gold leaf from the edges of the shape.

Making a rubber stamp

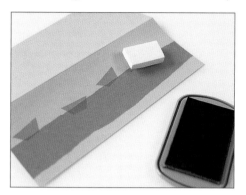

(see Bon voyage, page 94)

1 Either draw a freehand design onto the top of a soft, white eraser with a pencil, or trace around a card template.

2 Cut around the shape with a craft knife approximately 5 mm (⅛ in) into the eraser.

3 Slice away the excess eraser around the shape with the craft knife. For a more detailed stamp design you can use the same carving tools used for lino cutting. If the stamp shapes are very simple you can cut the whole shape from the eraser.

Making a lino cut

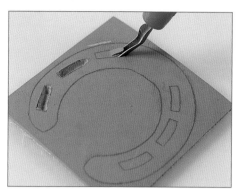

(see Good luck horseshoe, page 62)

1 Mark the design on the lino with a pencil by either transferring a template trace direct or by drawing around a template.

2 To make cutting in to the lino easier, warm the lino by leaving it on a radiator for 5 minutes or outside on a sunny day. Position the lino up against a wall or firm edge as this will prevent slipping when you cut out the lino. Score around the design with a craft knife.

3 Use different width blades in a lino cutter, such as a wide blade for cutting out large areas and a fine blade for more detailed areas, and cut out the design. The lino cut is now ready to be inked for printing.

Appliqué stitches

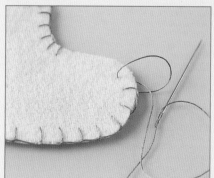

You can secure fabric pieces to card with spray adhesive or PVA glue, but to complete the card with a decorative finish you can't beat these simple, traditional stitches.

Blanket stitch (see above) Hold the side that you are working on towards you. Starting from the left, bring the needle up through the fabric so that it catches the edge and is pointing towards you. Loop the thread over the needle then make the next stitch by bringing the needle back through the fabric approximately 5 mm (⅛ in) to the right. Continue working left to right along the edge of the fabric.

Running stitch Thread your needle with a length of embroidery thread or cotton. Take four or five even stitches together, then gently pull the thread through the fabric before taking another series of stitches.

Slip stitch Work from right to left along the folded edge of the fabric. Bring the needle up through the folded edge and back down into the background fabric at a slight angle. Bring the needle back up again about 5 mm (⅛ in) down from the previous stitch, through the folded edge and continue stitching at regular intervals.

making an envelope

Follow the instructions below to make your own envelopes. When you've finished, why not rubber stamp or stencil a design on the envelope, or add some sparkle with glitter? Or, try cutting out an address label using scalloped edge scissors, in a contrasting colour.

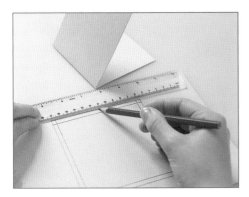

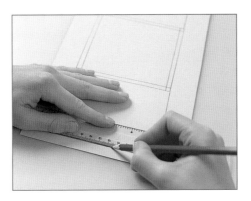

1 Make a template of your card by measuring out the finished, folded size on a piece of thin card, adding about 5 mm (⅛ in) to each edge. This is the front of the envelope.

2 Next, add the top flap on the upper edge, measuring half the depth of the front. Add the back on the lower edge, measuring the full size of the finished card, less about 2 cm (¾ in).

3 Add the side folds to each outer edge of the front, measuring 2.5 cm (1 in) wide. You can round off the corners if you prefer.

4 Cut out the template using sharp scissors and draw around it on your chosen paper or card. Fold the back and top flaps in to the centre and the side folds inwards.

5 Open out the flaps and either apply a thin layer of PVA glue to the side flaps or a strip of double-sided tape and seal the edges. Either tuck the top flap in or seal with double-sided tape or a fun sticker.

Traditional holidays and festivities give you the opportunity to make special handmade cards for family and friends. In this section you will find a broad selection of Christmas-themed cards that will suit all ages, together with hand-painted silk eggs or a cute fluffy bunny for Easter greetings and a Shaker-style Thanksgiving card. The cards use simple collage and 3-D effects together with sparkly glitter and gold leaf which are perfect for seasonal greetings.

Festive

fun

bobbing snowmen

These plump little snowmen are attached to the card background with a wire spiral, so that they can spring forwards and merrily bob up and down.

Materials
1 A5 sheet of deep purple card

1 sheet of A5 white card

1 sheet of pink metallic card (for a hat)

1 sheet of gold paper (for a hat and scarf)

Assorted small coloured sequins

Snowflake rubber stamp

White ink pad

White embossing powder

PVA glue

20-cm (8-in) length of jewellery wire

Fine tip black pen

Equipment
Scissors

Toaster

Pencil

Glue gun

Templates   Page 112

What to do

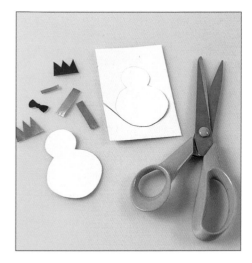

1 Fold the purple card in half and open out flat. Stamp the snowflake design all over the card with white ink. Re-apply ink to the stamp for each print.

2 Sprinkle the white embossing powder over each stamped snowflake and shake off the excess. Immediately hold the stamped snowflakes over a heat source, such as a toaster, until the powder melts.

3 Trace the snowmen templates onto white card and cut them out. Cut out the shapes for the hat, bow tie and scarf from the different coloured papers.

4 With a dab of PVA glue, stick the hats, scarf and sequins onto the snowmen. Draw the facial details with a black fine tip pen

5 Cut the length of wire in half. Coil each piece around a pencil to make a spiral. Glue one end of the wire to the reverse of the snowman just below the head with a hot glue gun. Glue a small piece of white card over the fixing point. Repeat for the second snowman.

6 Decide where you want to position the snowmen and mark the spot with a pencil. Apply a generous amount of glue from a hot gun, glue to the spot and then attach the wire. Support the wire while the glue dries. Repeat for the second snowman.

spinning star

The origami papers used in this design create an optical effect as the star spins. If you can't find the same ones, use any patterned papers in a common colour theme.

Materials

1 A5 sheet of red card

1 A4 sheet of thin card

1 sheet of striped paper (10.5 x 15 cm/4¼ x 7½ in)

PVA glue

1 sheet of red card (15 x 15 cm/ 6 x 6 in)

2 sheets of different patterned origami paper (15 x 15 cm/6 x 6 in)

Red thread

Adhesive tape

Equipment

Pencil

Scissors

Craft knife

Cutting mat

Glue brush

Fabric scissors

Needle

Templates   Page 112

What to do

1 Fold the red card in half. Photocopy or trace the star and circle templates onto the thin card and cut out with scissors.

2 Position the circle template on the inside front of the card, approximately 2.5 cm (1 in) from the top, and draw around with a pencil. Cut out the circle with a craft knife.

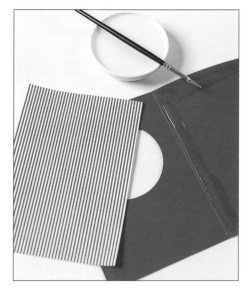

3 Apply PVA glue to the inside, right-hand page of the card and stick the piece of striped paper on top.

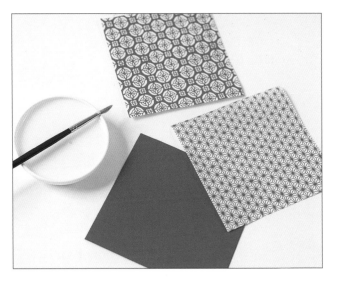

4 Stick the patterned paper squares to each side of the square of red card with PVA glue.

5 Position the star template in the centre of the patterned square and trace with a pencil. Cut out the star with a craft knife.

6 Thread the needle with a length of red thread and attach the star in the round window by piercing a hole in the top point of the star and again in the red card. Secure the thread with adhesive tape.

3-D snow scene

With a few simple folds and some adhesive tape, this 3-D card is easy to assemble. You could add snowmen in place of the trees for variation.

Materials
1 A5 sheet of blue card
1 A5 sheet of thin white card
1 A5 sheet of thin green metallic card
Silver glitter
White fine glitter
PVA glue
Double-sided tape

Equipment
Pencil
Old ballpoint pen or embossing tool
Glue brush
Snowflake paper punch
Scissors

Templates Page 113

What to do

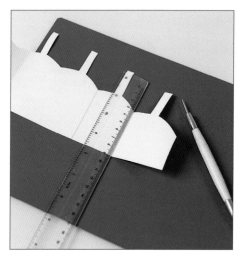

1 Fold the blue card in half. Photocopy or trace the snow scene and Christmas tree templates. Draw around the snow scene template on the white card and the Christmas trees on the green card, then cut out.

2 Score along the fold lines on the snow scene (see template) with an old ballpoint pen or embossing tool and fold them back.

3 Glue the Christmas trees onto the tabs of the snow scene using a small dab of PVA glue.

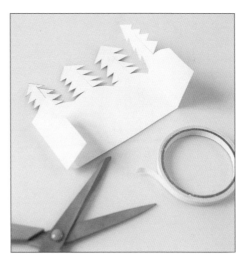

4 Brush PVA glue over the white card and sprinkle on the silver glitter, avoiding the tab on the far right. Shake off the excess.

5 Attach a strip of double-sided tape on the reverse of the left-hand side of the snow scene, another strip on the reverse side along the inside edge of the first fold, and one strip along the front edge of the last fold. Attach to the blue card.

6 Punch out white card snowflakes and brush with PVA glue. Sprinkle the snowflakes with white glitter, then shake off the excess and leave to dry.

7 Glue the snowflakes on the inside of the blue card behind the snow scene, and a few on the outside.

golden reindeer

This cute little reindeer has a bright, shiny nose. There is space at the bottom to add a Christmas greeting in a matching metallic pen, if you wish.

Materials
1 A4 sheet of thin card
1 sheet of burgundy card
   (10 x 10 cm/4 x 4 in)
PVA glue
Gold leaf metal
Red sequin
1 sheet of burgundy card
   (20 x 10 cm/8 x 4 in)
Adhesive foam pad

Equipment
Pencil
Craft knife
Cutting mat
Gue brush
Soft brush

Template   Page 114

What to do

1 Trace the reindeer template onto thin card and cut out. Trace around the template on the smaller piece of burgundy card and cut out with a craft knife.

2 Apply PVA glue to the cut out reindeer with a glue brush.

3 Position the gold leaf over the reindeer and smooth down with a dry brush. Dust away any excess leaf.

4 Glue the red sequin to the reindeer's nose with a dab of PVA glue.

5 Fold the burgundy card in half. Attach a foam pad to the reverse of the reindeer and stick it the centre of the card.

christmas cracker

A great card to send from the whole family as there is plenty of space for everyone to write a personal festive message.

Materials

1 sheet of green card (11 x 50 cm/ 4½ x 20 in)

1 sheet of purple paper (6.5 x 50 cm/2½ x 20 in)

A5 sheet of red paper (6.5 x 6.5 cm/2½ x 2½ in)

PVA glue

2 sheets of pink tissue paper (6.5 x 17 cm/2½ x 6½ in)

Sequins

Star stickers

Equipment

Embossing tool

Scalloped edge scissors

Glue brush

Scissors

Templates   Page 114

What to do

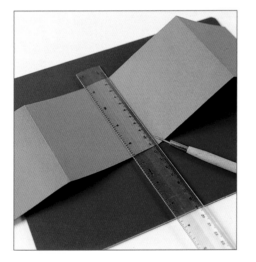

1 Mark three folds on the green card with an embossing tool and fold into four sections to create a concertina (see page 13).

2 Trace or photocopy the cracker templates and cut out the bands in red using scalloped edge scissors along the sides. Draw around the cracker end template on each end of the strip of purple paper and cut out.

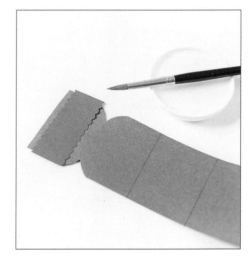

3 Mark three folds on the purple paper with an embossing tool and fold into four sections to match the green card. Glue the red paper shapes onto the purple cracker with PVA glue.

4 Trim the edges of the pieces of tissue paper with the scalloped edge scissors then scrunch up the tissue paper so that they look gathered. Glue each piece behind either end of the cracker.

5 Decorate the cracker with sequins and star stickers, using small dabs of PVA glue applied with a brush.

6 Glue the cracker onto the background card with PVA glue.

silk painted eggs

Silk paints are easy to apply and allow you the freedom to add your own exclusive design.

Materials

1 sheet of lilac card (30 x 9 cm/ 12 x 3½ in)

1 A4 sheet of thin card

1 sheet of lilac card (15 x 9 cm/ 16 x 3½ in)

Piece of white silk (15 x 7.5 cm/ 6 x 3 in)

1 sheet of thin card (16 x 12 cm/ 6¼ x 4¾ in)

Gutta/resist fluid in pink and gold

Silk paint in different colours

Masking tape

Double-sided tape

Equipment

Craft knife

Cutting mat

Pencil

Paint brush

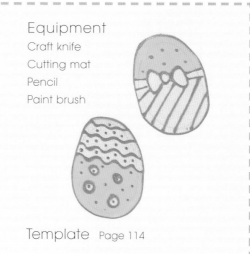

Template   Page 114

What to do

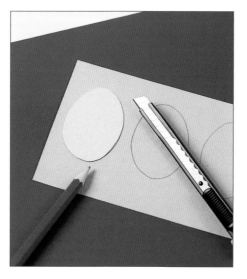

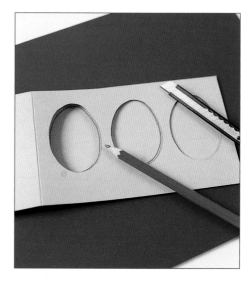

1 Fold the larger piece of lilac card in half. Photocopy or trace the egg template and cut out from the piece of thin card.

2 Draw around the egg template on the reverse of the front of the lilac card to make a row of three eggs. Cut out the eggs with a craft knife.

3 Place the smaller piece of lilac card behind the eggs and draw the outline of the eggs on the lilac card with a pencil, then cut out the eggs. The stencil shape will be added later to conceal the surrounding silk inside the card.

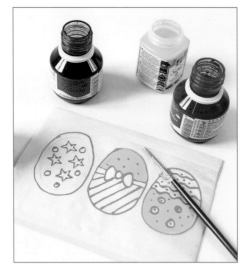

4 Tape the piece of silk to the slightly larger piece of thin card. Place the greeting card over the silk and very lightly draw around the eggs with a pencil onto the silk.

5 Outline the egg designs by applying the pink gutta/resist tube tip in a sufficiently thick and continuous line. Use the gutta/resist to outline patterns and shapes in pink and gold. Allow to dry for at least an hour.

6 Paint each colour of silk paint onto the chosen area of the design. Rinse and dry the brush well in between colours. You can re-apply colours to create deeper tones. Allow the paint to dry for one hour.

7 Remove the silk from the backing card. Tape the design behind the egg windows with masking tape. To finish, stick the lilac backing card stencil over the reverse of the design with double-sided tape.

pom-pom bunny

This sweet Easter bunny will appeal to adults and children alike. Vary the colours or increase the number of bunnies for an alternative design.

Materials

1 A5 sheet of yellow card

1 sheet of thin card
(10.5 x 10.5 cm/4½ x 4½ in)

1 piece of pink and white spot fabric
(10.5 x 10.5 cm/4½ x 4½ in)

Spray adhesive

Scraps of fabric for the bunting

PVA glue

Adhesive foam pads

Pink pom-pom

Equipment

Small scissors

Pencil

Glue brush

Coloured pencil

Glue gun

Templates Page 115

What to do

1 Fold the yellow card in half. Cut out a square of thin card and fabric (10.5 x 10.5 cm/4½ x 4½ in).

2 Spray adhesive over the front of the thin card and smooth the fabric on top.

3 Photocopy or trace the bunny and bunting templates and cut them out. Trace around the bunny template on the reverse of the spotty fabric and cut out with small scissors. Trace around the bunting template on four scraps of fabric and cut them out.

4 Glue the bunting in place along the top of the card and draw a coloured pencil line to link them together.

5 Apply two adhesive pads on the reverse of the bunny and stick onto the card. Fix the pom-pom tail with a hot glue gun.

thanksgiving shaker-style

This Shaker-style design is perfect for Thanksgiving wishes, but could easily be adapted for an anniversary card.

Materials

1 A5 sheet of white card

1 sheet of wood effect paper (10.5 x 15 cm/4½ x 6 in)

2 A5 sheets of thin card

2 pieces of different coloured check fabric (approximately 21 x 15 cm/8¼ x 6 in)

2 heart buttons

Spray adhesive

PVA glue

Equipment

Scissors

Pencil

Glue gun

Templates   Page 115

What to do

1 Fold the piece of white card in half. Photocopy or trace the shaker templates onto thin card then cut them out.

2 Glue the piece of wood effect paper to the front of the folded white card.

3 Spray adhesive on the reverse of the fabric shapes and stick them onto the thin card.

4 Draw around the templates on the reverse of the fabric and cut out.

5 Use PVA glue to stick the fabric shapes onto the card and glue a heart button onto each character with a hot glue gun.

gallery of festive cards

▶Pretty in pink This funky festive card is made using a piece of devouré velvet. Tiny silver beads add the finishing touch. Try different patterns for other occasions.
Kim Robertson

▶Animal magic A simple idea, but really effective: fake fur material has been glued onto the card base and a reindeer made from cut-out antlers, wobbly eyes and a sparkly red nose.
The Monster Factory

▶Branching out Another version of the Christmas tree but this designer has used green felt and textured papers to create the effect, with a length of gold wire to add a decorative finish.
Caroline Gardner

◀Starry, starry night A simple star is given an unusual twist – its outline has been created using pretty beads threaded onto wire and twisted into shape. It sits in a little plastic pocket for added impact.
Caroline Gardner

▶**Fairy dust** A printed artwork is glued onto a foam square and framed by a delicate piece of paper. The artwork has been carefully torn to create an interesting border. You could use pictures from magazines to recreate this effect.
Abigail Mill

◀**Christmas stocking** A mini knitted stocking on tiny wooden needles makes this a really eye-catching card. Silver thread finishes off the red wool and a gold star has been stuck on the for extra festive appeal.
Pearl and Black

▼**Snow storm** This pretty devouré velvet snowflake design has a wonderful, shimmering effect when the fabric catches the light.
Kim Robertson

▼**Sew special** Delicate needlework and sumptuous colours are added to an embroidered fabric rectangle which overlaps another of slightly different dimensions. Gold thread picks out the border of the tree.
Pearl and Black

▲Funny bunny This unusual take on the Easter bunny uses printing and embroidery in the design. A piece of handmade paper, a length of ribbon and a button make it really individual.
Rachel Coleman

▲Groovy chick Here's a great card for kids, as the big shapes are easy to cut. Yellow felt makes the shape of the chick with gold metallic paper forming the cracked egg.
Leigh Jones

▶Metallic egg Lots of different layers are used: shimmering fabric makes the backdrop, followed by a smaller piece of red felt, then the egg from metallic paper which is decorated with metallic paint and paper flowers.
Kathryn Ferrier

▶Easter cross The traditional Easter symbol is classically recreated using gold thread, which is embroidered onto a separate piece of card and glued onto the front. This design could also be used for Christmas cards.
Pearl and Black

▼Flower power A simple piece of patterned paper is used to maximum effect here. Save interesting wrapping paper or wallpaper off-cuts to make similar cards.
Katie Heester

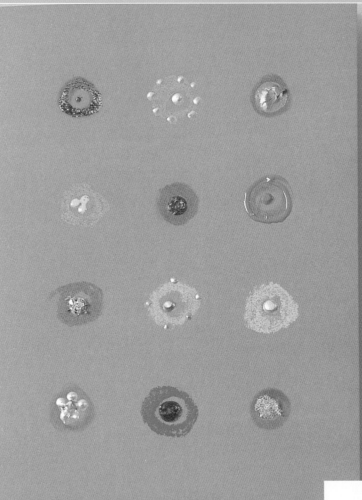

▲Paint effects Crayons, paint, glitter and a little imagination are all that's needed for this colourful card. Experiment with your own combination of colours and shapes, for different occasions.
Camilla Hall for White Space Designs

▶Glitterati Little printed designs are combined with metallic stars on a backing of tracing paper on this card that stands out from the crowd. Pick images that relate to particular occasions.

▲Classic kitsch This unusual design combines a patterned, glossy cover with a little cardboard lantern that swings from the top of the card by a length of gold thread. Pink string has been folded and stuck on the back to create tassels.
Petra Boase

Engagement, wedding, new baby, new home, anniversary, Mother's Day and Father's Day – all great excuses for making a card and joining in the celebrations. The cards in this section use a variety of techniques, from a layered fabric wedding cake to appliqué felt shapes, and simple wire work with stylish embellishments. For stitchers, the needlepoint house is an unusual idea with which to welcome friends to a new home. The Father's Day card can be adapted to suit any occasion and the patterned love heart lends itself to Valentine's day, engagement, wedding or anniversary wishes.

Celebr

ations

wedding cake

You can always add a personal touch to this design by writing the name of the couple and the date of their special day on the card.

Materials

1 sheet of cream card (30 x 15 cm/ 12 x 6 in)

1 A4 sheet of thin card

1 sheet of pale pink tracing paper (13 x 13 cm/5 x 5 in)

Spray adhesive

1 sheet of thick white card (13 x 13 cm/5 x 5 in)

13-cm (5-in) square of old pink cotton lace fabric

20-cm (8-in) length of old pink lace trim

Double-sided tape

PVA glue

16 gold sequins

2 white dove cake decorations

Equipment

Scissors

Pencil

Ruler

Glue gun

Templates Page 115

What to do

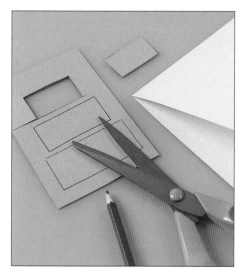

1 Fold the cream card in half. Trace or photocopy the cake templates onto thin card and cut out.

2 Spray adhesive on the reverse of the tracing paper and fix in the centre on the front of the card.

3 Spray adhesive on the thick white card and when tacky, smooth on the lace fabric.

4 Draw around the cake templates on the lace card and cut out. Cut lengths of lace trim to fit each shape and attach with a thin strip of double-sided tape.

5 Glue the cake pieces onto the greeting card with a 5-mm (⅛-in) gap inbetween each layer.

6 To finish, glue the sequins onto the cake pieces and glue the doves onto the top of the cake with a hot glue gun.

confetti church

This design can be adapted in many ways: you could use real confetti or dried rose petals; or vary the window shape – a heart or wedding cake would look perfect too.

Materials

1 A5 sheet of white card

1 A4 sheet of thin card

1 sheet of lilac card (10.5 x 15 cm/ 4¼ x 6 in)

1 A5 sheet of acetate

Selection of small novelty sequins

Masking tape

Double-sided adhesive tape

Equipment

Cutting mat

Craft knife

Scissors

Pencil

Template   Page 116

What to do

1 Fold the white card in half. Trace or photocopy the church template onto thin card and cut out.

2 Place the church template on the inside of the front of the card and draw around it.

3 Cut out the church with a craft knife on a cutting mat.

4 Place the piece of lilac card behind the church and draw the outline of the church onto the lilac card, then cut out the church shape with a craft knife. This will be added later to finish off the card.

5 Cut out two pieces of acetate measuring 10 x 11.5 cm (4 x 4¾ in). Tape the two pieces together with masking tape leaving one side open. Fill the acetate pocket with the sequins and secure the open end with masking tape.

6 Fix the acetate pocket to the inside of the card behind the cut-out church with double-sided tape. To finish the card, stick the lilac church cut-out behind the church with double-sided tape.

diamond ring

This is an engagement card with extra sparkle! For a wedding card, simply use the gold band and add a hand-written message in metallic gold ink.

Materials

1 A5 sheet of stencil card
1 sheet of pale pink card
   (21 x 10.5 cm/8¼ x 4¼ in)
Spray adhesive
Silver glitter
Tiny gold beads
PVA glue

Equipment

Pencil
Craft knife
Cutting mat
Glue brush
Scissors
Pencil

Template   Page 116

What to do

1 Trace the ring template onto stencil card and cut out with a craft knife to make the stencil. Keep the centre of the ring.

2 Fold the pink card in half. Spray adhesive on the reverse of the stencil and the centre of the ring and position both stencils on the front of the card.

3 With the glue brush, apply a generous amount of PVA glue to the stencil ring shape.

4 Carefully sprinkle the silver glitter so that it sticks to the jewel part of the ring. Lightly press down.

5 Apply more glue and sprinkle the beads over the band part of the ring then shake off the excess beads and glitter. Leave to dry for approximately half an hour.

6 Carefully remove the stencils to reveal the sparkling ring.

baby bootee

The perfect new baby card. Here, the baby's initial is stamped on the little tag, but you could write the baby's full name instead. For a little girl's version use pink tones.

Materials

1 sheet of cream card (30 x 15 cm/
  12 x 6 in)
1 A4 sheet of thin card
Cream wool or felt (10 x 10 cm/
  4 x 4 in)
Fine blue embroidery thread
8-cm (3-in) length of blue ribbon
Pale blue card for the tag
  (3 x 2 cm/1½ x 1 in)
Alphabet rubber stamps
Blue ink pad
Cream button
Patterned paper (10 x 9 cm/4 x 3¾ in)
PVA glue

Equipment

Pencil
Scissors
Fabric scissors
Needle
Ruler
Glue gun
Glue brush

Templates   Page 116

What to do

1 Fold the cream card in half. Trace or photocopy the bootie and tag templates onto thin card and cut them out.

2 Trace around the bootie template on the cream wool and cut out with fabric scissors.

3 Blanket stitch (see page 14) around the edge of the bootee using the blue embroidery thread.

4 Wrap the ribbon around the top of the bootee and glue in place on the reverse with a glue gun.

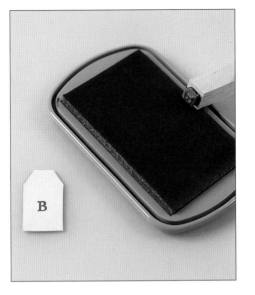

5 Cut out the tag from the pale blue card and using a rubber stamp, stamp on the baby's initial.

6 Glue the tag onto the front of the bootee and glue on the button with a hot glue gun.

7 Cut out the patterned paper for the background and glue it onto the card with PVA glue. Finally, glue on the bootie with a hot glue gun.

baby patchwork

A personalized welcome to the world. This delightful card uses simple stitches and would suit newborn baby wishes or a Christening or naming ceremony.

Materials

1 A5 sheet of mint green card

1 sheet of thin card (10.5 x 15 cm/ 4¼ x 6 in)

1 A5 piece of cream felt

Assorted cotton threads

Assorted buttons, sequins

Double-sided tape

Equipment

Pencil

Ruler

Scissors

Needle

What to do

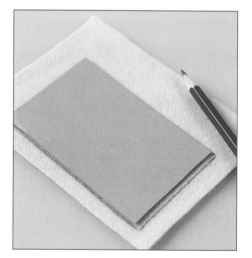

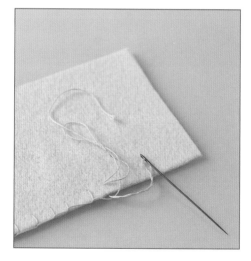

1 Fold the sheet of white card in half. Cut out a rectangle of thin card, 7 x 10.5 cm (3 x 4¼ in). You may have to adjust the sizes of the pieces of card according to how many letters the baby's name has.

2 Trace around the card rectangle on the felt and cut out with scissors.

3 Thread the needle with blue thread and blanket stitch (see page 14) around the edge of the piece of felt.

4 Attach the buttons and sequins with thread in two rows along the top and bottom of the felt rectangle.

5 With pink thread, use simple stitches to add the baby's name, keeping the letters evenly spaced.

6 Attach the felt panel to the card with double-sided tape.

new home

Modelling clay is ideal for simple decorations and is available in a huge range of colours, together with pearlescent and glow-in-the-dark varieties.

Materials
1 A5 sheet of green card
Modelling clay in two colours, such as white and silver
1 A5 sheet of bronze paper
PVA glue
1 A4 sheet of white paper
Bird charms or sequins

Equipment
Small rolling pin
Oven
Glue gun
Glue brush
Craft knife

Template   Page 117

What to do

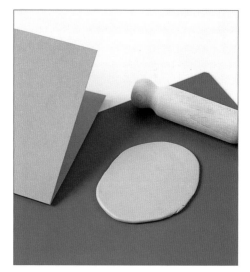

1 Fold the green card in half. Roll out a small ball of silver modelling clay the size of a walnut with a small rolling pin, until it is approximately 5 mm (⅛ in) thick. This is the background.

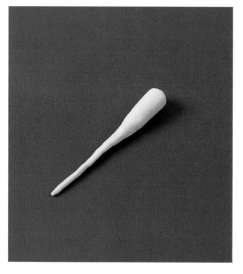

2 Roll another small ball of clay in the second colour into a continuous rolled strip, until it is approximately 5 mm (⅛ in) thick.

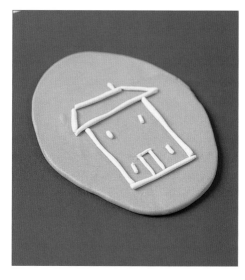

3 Cut the rolled strip into different length pieces to make up the shape of a house. Position the strips on the clay background and press down lightly.

4 Working in one direction only, roll over the design with the small rolling pin – the house shape will sink into the background clay to make a smooth surface.

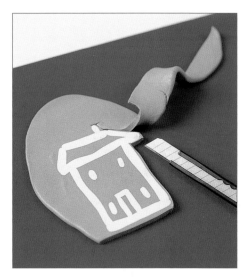

5 Cut around the outline of the house leaving a narrow border of the background colour.

6 Bake the clay shape following the instructions on the clay packet. Once baked and cooled, stick the house onto the folded card background with a hot glue gun.

7 Make a fence from thin strips of bronze paper and attach with PVA glue. Trace the cloud template onto white paper and cut out. Attach the cloud and bird charms to the sky with PVA glue to finish the card.

needlepoint house

This is the perfect portable project to do in the evenings, on your travels or simply while chatting to friends.

Materials

Interlock canvas 12 count
(13 x 13 cm/5¼ x 5¼ in)

Sheet of tracing paper

Tapestry wool in green, grey, brown, pink, turquoise, yellow

1 sheet of blue card (30 x 15 cm/ 12 x 7½ in)

1 sheet of blue card (15 x 15 cm/ 7½ x 7½ in)

Masking tape

Double-sided tape

Equipment

Tapestry needle

Cutting mat

Craft knife

Metal edge ruler

Scissors

Needlepoint chart   Page 117

What to do

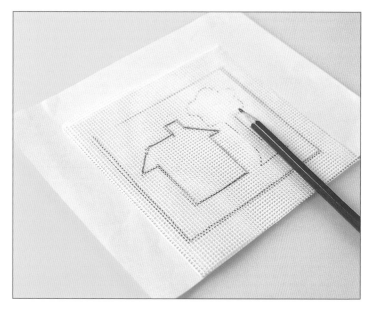

1 To transfer the design onto your canvas, first trace the outlines onto tracing paper with a dark pencil. Place the tracing under the canvas and overdraw the tracing with a pencil. Alternatively, you can count the stitches from the chart to follow the pattern.

2 Stitch the design with a classic half-cross stitch following the colour chart. Work each row from left to right, but don't stitch the windows.

3 Fold the larger piece of blue card in half. Place the card opened out on a cutting mat and mark out the window mount to measure 10 x 9 cm (4 x 3½ in), centred 4 cm (1½ in) from the bottom of the card. Cut out with a craft knife and metal edge ruler.

4 Position the finished tapestry behind the window mount and secure in place with masking tape.

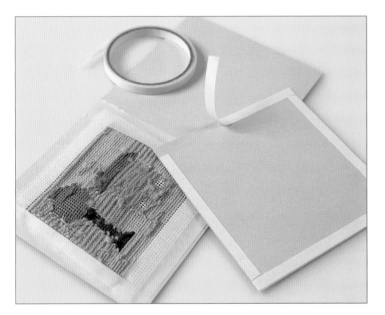

5 To conceal the back of the needlepoint, attach the smaller piece of blue card on the reverse with double-sided tape.

mother's day wire flowers

An extra special bouquet of flowers that won't need watering – perfect for Mother's Day!

Materials

1 sheet of mint green card (22 x 19 cm/8½ x 7½ in)

1 A4 sheet of thin card

1 sheet of lilac card (8 x 8 cm/3 x 3 in)

30-cm (12-in) length of fine green wire

4 pieces of felt in different colours, such as pale pink, pink, pale turquoise, green (5 x 5 cm/ 2 x 2 in each)

Gold paper doily

Button

Ribbon rosebud

Sequin

Spray adhesive

Adhesive tape

Equipment

Glue gun

Scissors

Ruler

Templates   Page 117

What to do

1 Fold the mint green card in half. Trace or photocopy the flower, leaf and flower pot templates onto thin card and cut out.

2 Draw around the flower and leaf templates on the reverse of the pieces of felt and the flower pot template on the lilac card and cut out the shapes.

3 Spray adhesive on a piece of gold doily and smooth it onto the flower pot. Cut away the excess.

4 Glue a button, rosebud and sequin in the centre of each of the felt flowers with a hot glue gun.

5 Cut three lengths of wire 10 cm (4 in) each and glue each one behind a flower. Glue a leaf onto each wire in a different position with a hot glue gun.

6 Decide on your flower arrangement and stick the wires to the back of the flower pot with tape at the base of the stems. Apply glue just on the reverse of the flower pot and stick on the card.

father's day photo card

Surprise your Dad with this card by sliding a dashing snap of the two of you in the frame. And for new Dads, what could be better than a photo of their little angel?

Materials

1 A5 sheet of blue card

1 A4 sheet of thin card

1 A4 sheet of thin gold card

Gold paper doily

1 sheet of acetate (21 x 10.5 cm/ 8¼ x 4¼ in)

Spray adhesive

Adhesive tape

Double-sided tape

Equipment

Craft knife

Cutting mat

Pencil

Scissors

Templates   Page 118

What to do

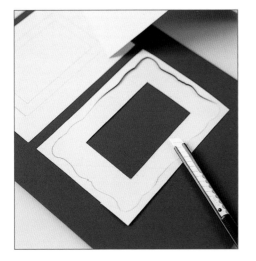

1 Fold the blue card in half. Trace or photocopy the frame templates onto thin card and cut out.

2 Draw around the frame templates on the reverse of the gold card and cut out.

3 Cut strips of the gold doily to cover the main frame. Spray adhesive on the reverse of the pieces and smooth them in place on the frame. Cut away the excess doily.

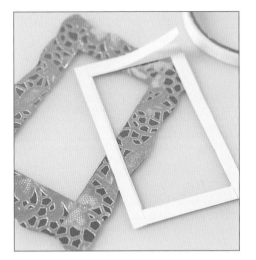

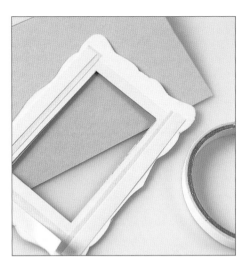

4 Stick double-sided tape on the reverse of the inner frame and stick it in place on the main frame.

5 Attach the piece of acetate behind the inner frame with strips of adhesive tape.

6 Cut three strips of double-sided tape and stick them along the bottom and sides of the frame. Stick the frame on the card.

7 Cut your photograph to size and slide it in the frame.

embossed tin love heart

This card uses a few simple tools and materials for an impressive result that would make a perfect greeting to mark a wedding or anniversary.

Materials

1 sheet of pale pink card (24 x 24 cm/9½ x 9½ in)

1 A4 sheet of paper

Metal embossing foil (14 x 14 cm/ 5½ x 5½ in)

Equipment

Embossing tool or ballpoint pen

Soft embossing mat or surface

Scissors

Pencil

Masking tape

Glue gun

Template   Page 119

What to do

1 Fold the pale pink card in half. Trace or photocopy the heart template and patterns onto the paper and cut out.

2 Tape the heart template to the piece of embossing foil with masking tape.

3 Draw over the design on the template with an embossing tool or ballpoint pen.

4 Remove the heart template and cut around the heart with scissors.

5 Glue the metal heart onto the pink card using a hot glue gun.

champagne congratulations

With its slightly retro style, this card is perfect for sending engagement or anniversary wishes to any modern couple. Practise manipulating the metal wire before you begin.

Materials

60-cm (24-in) length of thin pink metal wire plus extra for practising

Pencil

1 sheet of black card (30 x 15 cm/ 12 x 6 in)

1 sheet of pink paper (10 x 10 cm/ 4 x 4 in)

Strong glue

PVA glue

Silver sequins

Gold or silver pen

Equipment

Jewellery pliers

Needle

Eraser

Templates   Page 119

What to do

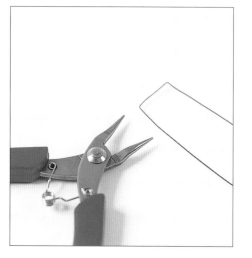

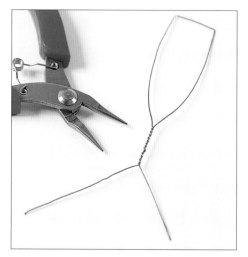

1 Cut the length of wire in half as each glass uses 30 cm (12 in) of wire. Find the centre of the wire, clamp with a pair of jewellery pliers and bend one side to 90 degrees.

2 Measure along 2 cm (¾ in) and bend another right angle to make the top of the glass.

3 Cross the wires 7 cm (2¾ in) from the top of the glass and clamp tightly with the pliers. Twist the ends of the wires to make the stem of the glass approximately 2 cm (¾ in) long.

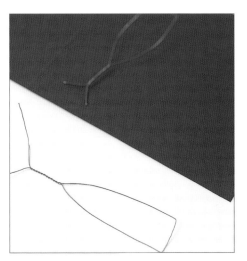

4 Shape the body of the glass with your fingers. Bend each end of the wire at the base of the glass by 1.5 cm (½ in).

5 Fold the piece of black card in half. Position each glass on the card background and mark on the card with a pencil where the wire will be pierced through.

6 Make a small hole in the card with a needle. Pierce the wire through the holes and fold back on the inside of the card. Repeat Steps 1–6 for the second glass.

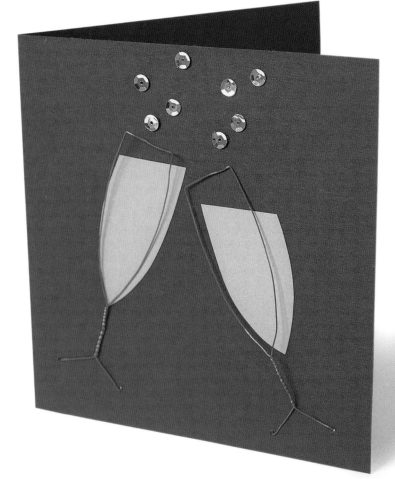

7 Cut out glass shapes from the pink paper using the template and glue behind the glasses with PVA glue. Glue sequin champagne bubbles above the clinking glasses. Write your message inside the card with a gold or silver pen.

good luck horseshoe

Lino cutting is ideal for printing multiple cards as you simply reapply the ink for each print.

Materials
Tracing paper
Lino board
Purple water-based ink
1 sheet of white card (20 x 10 cm/ 8 x 4 in)
1 sheet of tissue paper (10 x 10 cm/ 4 x 4 in)
Fine red glitter
Spray adhesive

Equipment
Pencil
Lino cutters
Craft knife
Piece of hardboard or glass
Brayer (rubber covered roller)
Rolling pin
Scalloped edge scissors

Template   Page 119

What to do

1 Trace the horseshoe design onto a piece of tracing paper. Rub pencil over the reverse of the design.

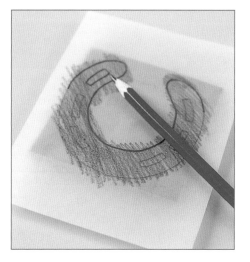

2 Position the tracing paper on the lino and draw over the pattern with a pencil. This will transfer the design onto the lino.

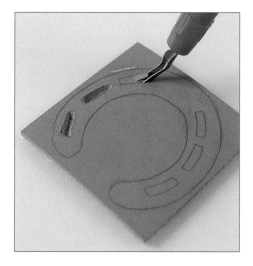

3 Warm the lino on a radiator or in the sunshine, to make scoring and cutting easier. Position the lino so that it butts up against a wall, such as the back of a kitchen work top – this will make cutting the lino easier and help prevent it slipping. Cut out the shape with lino cutters.

4 Squeeze a small amount of ink onto a piece of hardboard or glass. Disperse the ink evenly with the roller. Run the inked roller over the lino cut several times until all the raised lino is evenly covered with ink.

5 Cut a piece of tissue paper with scalloped edge scissors and lay it over the lino cut. Gently smooth it in place with a rolling pin.

6 Remove the tissue paper and sprinkle glitter over the print while the ink is still wet. Shake off the excess glitter and allow to dry.

7 Fold the card in half. Spray adhesive onto the tissue paper and stick to the front of the card.

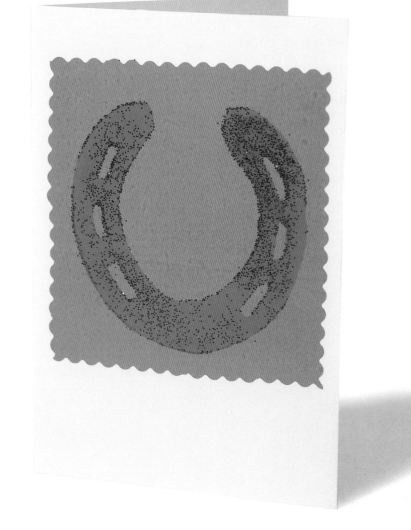

gallery of celebration cards

◄**Romantic gesture** This beaded heart is surrounded by a faint border of pencil-drawn hearts and cut-out designs of a butterfly and a flower. A silver star has been stuck on the top and the end result is unusual and pretty.
Rosie Marshall

▲**Wedding bells** This delicate embroidered card has a gold thread design around a pink fabric wedding cake. A small velvet heart provides the finishing touch.
Abigail Mill

▲**White wedding** A church made from wire and ribbon, and drops of silver confetti make this an eye-catching wedding card. Wire can be used to make all kinds of shapes – try houses, numbers or engagement rings.
Pearl and Black

▶**Heart to heart** A pair of hearts cut from velvet material, sit on a pale fabric square and piece of gold ribbon. Gold embroidery picks out a cute pattern on the hearts and can be used in a similar way on different designs.
Vicky King

▶**A jewel of a card** This contemporary design uses foam shapes and printed designs. The heart has been decorated with a glass bead and smaller beads have been carefully sewn around the edges.
Rosie Marshall

◀**Simply stunning** A heart shape has been crafted from a piece of wire and sits inside a transparent plastic pocket – a simple idea with impact. Plastic pockets can be used to hold anything from beads to photos.
Caroline Gardner

◀**All that glitters** Pink fabric sits on top of gold mesh with a tiny gold heart in the middle. Gold sparkly dots and embroidery add detail to this intricate card.
Vicky King

◀**Elegant embroidery** This stunning card uses gold paper onto which a piece of see-through, patterned material has been stuck. An elaborate pattern has been embroidered around the edges and onto the red velvet heart that sits in the centre.
Abigail Mill

Celebrations **65**

◀Moving on Another example of a card where gold wire has been formed into a shape. The details of the windows and front door have been drawn on by hand.
Caroline Gardner

▼Raise the flag This quick and easy design uses a piece of stick and a triangle of cloth to make a flag. It's stuck onto squares of blue and yellow paper, which give this collage card a summer holiday feel.
Big Sky Designs

▲House of cards A pretty house has been created from pieces of fabric in different colours. Everything has been neatly stitched onto a separate fabric background, with a piece of embroidered ribbon at the base.
Vicky King

▲Charming card A rectangular piece of striped card in the centre has a variety of little plastic charms glued onto it, including a horseshoe for good luck. Look out for tiny objects that relate to special events and occasions.
Petra Boase

▼Ribbons and bows A watercolour picture sits on a pink fabric square on this card that welcomes the arrival of a new baby. Pink ribbon has been carefully threaded through the fold. *Pearl and Black*

►Out for a stroll Embroidery has been used to full effect, creating a pram against a yellow and blue backdrop. *Pearl and Black*

►Hanging by a thread This is a wonderfully unusual design that uses wire to create a little coat hanger to hold a pink knitted jumper decorated with ribbon. *Acorn Art*

▲It's a boy! The chequered blue background matches the little blue and white bow, whilst embroidery has been used to add features to the felt head. A touch of pink felt-tip pen is perfect for making rosy cheeks. *Petra Boase*

You can have lots of fun with birthday cards – pick a favourite topic or style and go to town! In this section you will find plenty of ideas for girl friends – a stand-alone handbag, appliqué cupcake for those with a sweet tooth, pressed flowers and even a party dress. The photo rosette provides endless opportunities for giving the birthday boy or girl a badge to remember.

Birth

day

handbag chic

Every woman loves a new handbag, so have fun making this for your friends using fabrics and colours you know they love to wear.

Materials

2 A4 sheets of thin card

1 A4 sheet of thick white card

2 A4 sheets of thin coloured card (to match your fabric)

1 piece of flowery fabric (20 x 15 cm/ 8 x 6 in)

Large flower sequin

Ribbon rosebud

Equipment

Glue gun

Glue brush

Scissors

Craft knife

Ruler

Pencil

Template   Page 120

What to do

 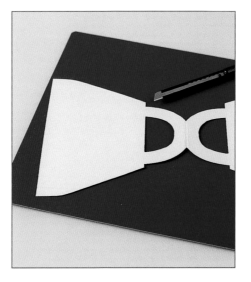 

1 Photocopy the handbag template onto a thin piece of card and cut out. Fold the thick card in half. Place the top of the handbag template along the fold line and draw around the rest of the bag.

2 Cut out the handbag shape. Open it out to reveal the front and back of the card.

3 Glue the flower fabric onto a piece of paper or thin card. When the glue has dried, draw around the template, excluding the handle, onto the fabric and cut out the shape. Glue the shape onto the front of the handbag card.

4 Draw around the handle part of the template, then draw a semi-circle for the flap on the matching coloured card.

5 Glue the handle and then the flap onto the card with PVA glue.

6 Glue the sequin and rosebud onto the bag using a hot glue gun.

diamanté disco cat

This cheeky jewelled cat is sure to put a smile on anyone's face. Reduce the size of the template and use different coloured felts for a card decorated with feline friends.

Materials

1 sheet of cream card (30 x 15 cm/ 12 x 6 in)

1 A4 sheet of thin card

1 sheet of pale blue tracing paper (12 x 12 cm/4¾ x 4¾ in)

Spray adhesive

Piece of cream wool or felt (10 x 10 cm/4 x 4 in)

4 x 9-cm (3½-in) strands of blue cotton yarn

Red embroidery thread

Small piece of pink felt for the nose

Small piece of pink fabric for the ears

Two craft eyes

6-cm (2¼-in) length of pink velvet ribbon

5 sequin jewels

Equipment

Scissors

Glue gun

Templates Page 120

What to do

1 Fold the cream card in half. Trace or photocopy the cat, ears and nose templates onto thin card and cut out.

2 Fix the piece of blue tracing paper to the front of the card with spray adhesive.

3 Cut out the cat shape from the cream wool. Position the strands of blue cotton on the face. Thread a needle with red embroidery thread and sew the yarns in place in the centre of the piece of felt.

4 Sew a line 1 cm (½ in) long down from the centre of the whiskers, and a 1 cm (½ in) stitch either side to create the cat's smile.

5 Cut out the fabric for the ears and felt for the nose and glue in place with a hot glue gun, then glue on the eyes.

6 Glue the velvet ribbon for the collar at the base of the neck, tucking the raw ends on the reverse. Glue the jewels on the velvet ribbon.

7 Stick the cat to the blue tracing paper background with a hot glue gun to finish.

embroidered cupcake

Almost edible, this is the perfect birthday card for any friend with a sweet tooth. This tasty appliqué cake is made with old scraps of fabric.

Materials
1 sheet of cream card (30 x 15 cm/ 12 x 6 in)

1 A4 sheet of thin card

Iron-on adhesive (15 x 15 cm/6 x 6 in)

Scraps of fabric to make up the cake (see templates for sizes)

7.5-cm (3-in) length of rik-rak braid

Assortment of different coloured machine threads

1 red button

Spray adhesive

Equipment
Craft knife

Cutting mat

Iron

Ironing board

Pencil

Needle

Scissors

Ruler

Templates   Page 121

What to do

1 Fold the cream card in half. Trace or photocopy the cake and background templates onto thin card and cut out.

2 On an ironing board, iron the iron-on adhesive on the reverse of the pieces of fabric, except for the background piece.

3 Draw around the templates on the backing paper with a pencil then cut out all the shapes including the background fabric. Peel off the protective backing paper from the cupcake shapes.

4 Assemble the cupcake on the background fabric and iron in place. Start with the cake, then add the icing and the paper case. Finally, add the length of rik-rak along the top of the paper case by sewing in place with a running stitch (see page 14).

5 Embroider the small cake decorations with different coloured small stitches and sew the button on the top of the cake.

6 Sew around the casing of the cake shape with simple slip stitches (see page 14).

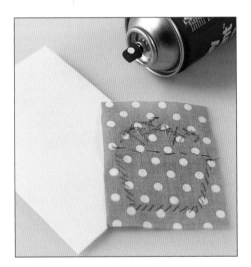

7 Spray adhesive on the reverse of the fabric and smooth in place on the front of the folded card.

oriental pressed flowers

You could use any seasonal flowers for this card. Rose petals, pansies, daisies and even lavender heads all press well. Press your flowers at least one week in advance.

Materials
1 sheet of cream card (21 x 10.5 cm/8¼ x 4¼ in)
Pressed flowers
Sheet of origami paper
PVA glue
Gold leaf

Equipment
Flower press
Glue brush
Soft brush

What to do

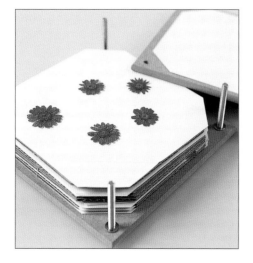

1 Pick fresh flowers from your garden at least one week before you make the card. Lay the petals or flower heads between sheets of paper in a flower press and close tightly. Leave in a cool, dry place for at least one week, preferably three, for a good result.

2 Fold the cream card in half. Cut a strip of origami paper 10.5 x 2.5 cm (4¼ x 1 in).

3 Glue the strip of origami paper off-centre on the front of the card with a glue brush and PVA glue.

4 Paint PVA glue on the reverse of the flowers and stick in place on the origami paper.

5 Dab tiny amounts of PVA glue on the origami paper and when tacky, smooth on small pieces of gold leaf with a soft brush. Brush away the excess gold leaf.

polka dot present

This design lends itself to an infinite variety of colour and pattern combinations. You could also adapt the idea to make a smaller card as a matching gift tag.

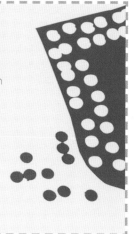

Materials
1 sheet of pink card (30 x 15 cm/
    12 x 6 in)
75-cm (30-in) length of stripey ribbon
Double-sided tape
1 A5 sheet of red card
PVA glue

Equipment
Scissors
Ruler
Round hole punch
Glue gun
Glue brush

What to do

1 Fold the pink card in half and cut the ribbon into the following lengths: 1 x 15 cm (6 in), 2 x 30 cm (12 in).

2 Stick the ribbon lengths across the present with double-sided tape.

3 Tie a bow using the remaining 30-cm (12-in) length of ribbon and stick to the card with a hot glue gun where the ribbons cross over.

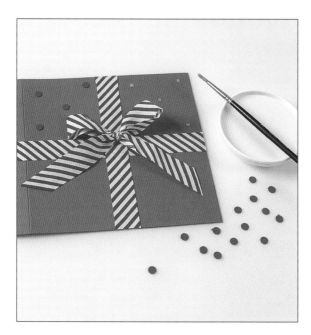

4 Punch lots of spots from red card and glue them onto the present in a random pattern with dabs of PVA glue.

stained glass flowers

This card glows when the light shines through the coloured tissue papers. It is suitable for any occasion and could easily be adapted for a wedding or christening.

Materials

1 sheet of tracing paper
(15 x 15 cm/6 x 6 in)

1 sheet of mint green card
(30 x 15 cm/12 x 6 in)

Selection of coloured tissue papers

PVA glue

Equipment

Pencil

Cutting mat

Craft knife or scalpel

Scissors

Fine glue brush

Ruler

Eraser

Templates   Page 122

What to do

1 Trace the flower template onto a piece of tracing paper. Rub pencil over the reverse of the design.

2 Fold the green card in half. Position the tracing paper on the inside front of the mint green card and draw over the pattern with a pencil. This will transfer the design onto the card.

3 Lay the card open on a cutting mat and carefully cut out the marked design with a craft knife or scalpel.

4 Cut out small pieces of colour tissue paper and glue them behind the flower shapes using PVA glue and a fine brush.

5 Overlap tissue paper colours and tones to create different effects, such as stripes. When the glue is dry fold the card in half.

photo fun rosette

You don't have to be a pet or come first in a show to wear a rosette – send this card to a friend to let them know you think they're the best!

Materials

A5 sheet of red card

1 sheet of thick white card
(10 x 10 cm/4 x 4 in)

Photograph

2.5-cm (1-in) wide pleated ribbon,
12 cm (4¾ in) long

2.5-cm (1-in) wide ribbon, 26 cm
(10 in) long

Badge pin

PVA glue

Equipment

Scissors

Glue brush

Pencil

Glue gun

Template Page 123

What to do

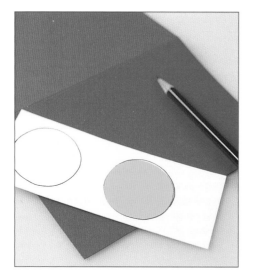

1 Fold the red card in half. Trace or photocopy the circle template twice onto the thick white card and cut out.

2 Use the circle template to cut out the photo and stick it onto one of the card circles.

3 Glue the pleated ribbon around the reverse of the card circle with the photograph on it using a hot glue gun.

4 Cut two lengths of wide ribbon to measure 13 cm (5 in) each. Stick these on the reverse of the second circle of card so that they overlap and splay out. Snip into the ends of the ribbon to create points.

5 Glue the two circles of card together. Glue a badge pin on the reverse of the rosette.

6 Pierce the badge pin through the front of the folded card to attach the rosette.

party girl

This pretty fabric design makes the perfect card for every girl friend or shopaholic.

Materials

1 A5 sheet of white card

1 A4 sheet of thin white card

2 pieces of fabric for the dress
  (see templates for size)

Double-sided tape

1 piece of interfacing
  (10.5 x 15 cm/4¼ x 6 in)

Pink machine thread

Butterfly sequin

Equipment

Fabric marker pen

Sewing machine

Scissors

Glue gun

Pencil

Templates   Page 122

What to do

1 Fold the white card in half. Trace or photocopy the dress templates onto thin card and cut out.

2 Trace around the templates on the fabric and cut out.

3 Stick a small piece of double-sided tape in the centre of each piece.

4 Stick the dress shapes on the front of the card.

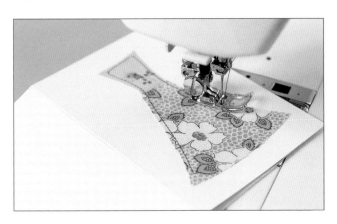

5 Place the piece of interfacing behind the dress on the inside of the card and sew around the dress with a straight running stitch, leaving approximately a 5-mm (⅛-in) border. Cut away any excess interfacing.

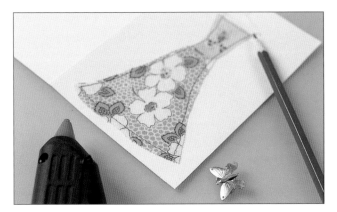

6 Attach the butterfly sequin to the centre of the dress with a hot glue gun and then draw a coat hanger with a pencil to finish.

gallery of birthday cards

▶**Cut the cake** A printed design of cakes and hearts has been artfully torn and glued onto a square of white tracing paper. Red glitter really brings the design to life. You can use glitter on cards for all occasions, but use sparingly.
Abigail Mill

▶**It's a gift** A piece of striped paper is made to look like a present on this birthday card. Sequins are used as decorations and a blue bow finishes off the gift.
Nosey Parker Cards for Pearl and Black

▶**Bee in your bonnet** A simple idea that can be adapted for different occasions: a rectangle of piece of floral-patterned paper has three bees glued along the centre. Try designing pictures on the computer then printing them out for your homemade cards.
Rosie Marshall

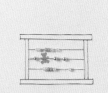

◀**Birthday countdown** This card uses a hand-drawn abacus design as its base. Little plastic beads have been threaded onto wires then carefully glued on, to finish it off.
Pearl and Black

▼Velvet crush On this tactile card, velvet ribbon has been wrapped around a piece of pink foam. It also includes stitching detail, beads and printed flower and cherub designs.
Rosie Marshall

◄Perfect print This brightly coloured foliage has been printed onto the actual card in this instance. You can buy special cards that feed into a printer so you can save your favourite designs and just print them out whenever you need a card.
Kim Robertson

◄Spot the difference This fun card combines spots and stripes in colourful contrast. The spotty background is printed onto the actual card and a little figurine is perched in the centre of a floral, cross-hatched square of paper.
Petra Boase

▲Say it with flowers This delicate design has a metallic card flower glued in the centre, with a piece of gauze below for the petals and silver wire for the stem.
Pearl and Black

◄Birthday This pretty design is based around an old postcard that has been customised with fabric flowers and printed cut-outs to give a modern twist. Why not re-use your old postcards or greetings cards and transform them into new designs?
Maud Hewlings

▲New look Again, an old postcard has been re-worked to create a new card with an oriental theme. Flower designs have been glued onto the card, as well as a fabric flower, a little pink bow and a decoration with a painting of a lady at its centre.
Maud Hewlings

►Dreamscape
Purple flower shapes have been printed onto a red card background and result in a wonderfully obscure pattern. There are many printing techniques that you can experiment with to create similar effects.
Kim Robertson

◄Pet project This innovative design has a printed patterned section on the front and a cut-out birdcage that swings on a piece of gold thread. A miniature bird trinket has been glued onto the cage as a final touch.
Petra Boase

◄Pass the parcel
Cardboard has been used to make the present here which is decorated with heart-shaped stamps and a red ribbon tied in a bow. There's also a little paper gift tag.
Jennifer Montgomery for Funky Eclectica

▲Naturally elegant
Here, the design has been printed directly onto card. The effect is simple but the colours really make it stand out. You could try and create a similar design using homemade stencils.
Kim Robertson

►Dressing up Little pieces of material cleverly create a glamorous dress, which sits on a hanger made from a piece of wire. Save your odds and ends of material and make your own designs.
Acorn Art

▲Air mail A miniature plastic bird delivers the post on this card. An envelope has been made from paper for the bird to carry, whilst a little pink ribbon and some silver wire have also been glued on to complete the picture.
Ilium at Pearl and Black

This section is full of ideas for general cards that you can adapt for any occasion, be it a birthday, anniversary, invitation, thank-you note or just to say hello. There aren't many crafters who don't have a box full of old scraps of fabric, ribbons, buttons and lace, not to mention leftover bits of paper, tissue paper, old magazine cuttings, photos, and embellishments. The Stripey paper fruit, Vintage collage and Button flower cards all make use of unwanted items or scraps to create a unique and fun card.

Everyday greet

ings

stripey paper fruit

Never have old wallpaper scraps looked so fruity. The more the patterns and colours clash, the better!

Materials

1 A5 sheet of white card

1 piece of spotty wallpaper (10.5 x 15 cm/4 x 6 in)

1 A4 sheet of white paper

Assorted sheets of coloured paper for the stripes (approximately 8 different colours)

1 A4 sheet of thin card

PVA glue

1 sheet of thick card (10 x 10 cm/ 4 x 4 in)

Green paper or wallpaper

Equipment

Scissors

Pencil

Cutting mat

Scalpel or craft knife

Metal edge ruler

Glue brush

Black marker pen

Templates Page 123

What to do

1 Fold the white card in half. Glue the spotty wallpaper onto the front of the card.

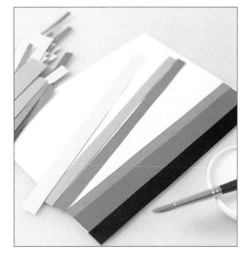

2 Cut lots of strips of coloured paper using a scalpel and metal ruler. Stick the strips onto a sheet of white paper.

3 Photocopy or trace the apple and pear templates onto thin card and cut them out. Draw around the fruit templates on the stripey paper and cut out.

4 Cut out the fruit shapes from thick card or cardboard.

5 Stick the stripey fruit shapes onto thick card fruits with PVA glue.

6 Stick the fruits to the front of the card. Cut out a small leaf shape from the green paper and stick onto the card, adding veins to the leaves with a black marker pen to finish.

bon voyage

This is a great way of making your own simple rubber stamps. You can vary the pattern and colours to suit a particular occasion.

Materials

1 sheet of blue card (19.5 x 16 cm/ 7¾ x 6¼ in)
1 sheet of blue tissue paper
Spray adhesive
Erasers
Rubber stamp ink pads in different colours
Scraps of fabric
PVA glue

Equipment

Craft knife
Cutting mat
Pencil
Glue brush

Templates   Page 124

What to do

1 Fold the pale blue card in half. Trace or photocopy the boat and sail templates onto thin card and cut out.

2 Tear a strip of blue tissue paper and stick it onto the card with spray adhesive. Trim away any excess tissue paper. Leave a small gap at the bottom of the card.

3 Draw around the boat templates on separate pieces of eraser and cut around the shape approximately 5 mm (⅛ in) deep into the rubber.

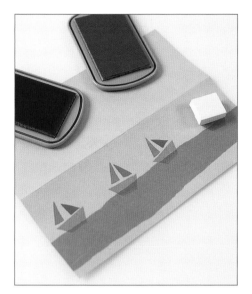

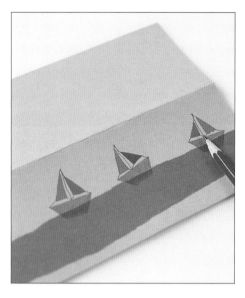

4 Dab the base of the boat shape on the ink pad and print four boats onto the card along the tissue paper band.

5 Apply the same method for the sails of the boats, varying their position and angles to give a feel of bobbing along, with different colour ink combinations.

6 Draw a mast on each boat using a pencil line, adding some rigging to join the sails.

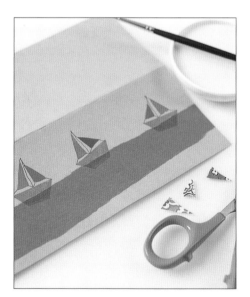

7 Cut out small triangles of fabric for the flags and stick in place at the top of the masts with PVA glue.

butterfly surprise

This card is a two-in-one design. First, you have the flowery card and then you can turn it inside out to reveal the fluttering butterfly.

Materials

1 A5 sheet of pale blue card

1 A4 sheet of thin card

Flowery paper, such as old wallpaper or wrapping paper

Assortment of sequins

1 A5 sheet of lilac card

Strong glue or glue gun

PVA glue

30-cm (12-in) length of 5 mm (⅛ in) blue ribbon

15-cm (6-in) length of fine green metallic wire

2 small beads

PVA glue

Equipment

Scissors

Glue brush

Needle

Template Page 124

What to do

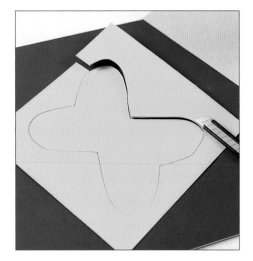

1 Fold the pale blue card in half. Trace or photocopy the butterfly template onto thin card and cut out.

2 Cut out lots of paper flowers from old wallpaper or wrapping paper. Glue two sequins onto the centre of each flower with a hot glue gun.

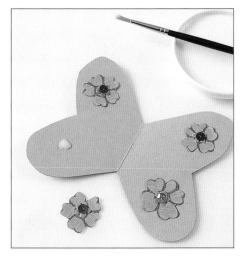

3 Trace around the butterfly template on the lilac card and cut out. Stick four of the sequin paper flowers onto the butterfly.

4 Thread a needle with the ribbon. Position the butterfly inside the card along the spine and sew in place with one long stitch.

5 Tie the end of the ribbon in a bow on the outside of the card and trim off the excess.

6 Decorate the front of the card by randomly sticking on the paper flowers and sequin shapes with PVA glue.

vintage collage

A great project for anyone who loves collecting old postcards, nostalgia, old fabrics and quirky charms.

Materials
1 A5 sheet of white card

Vintage postcard

PVA glue

Collage pieces from old magazines, brochures, newspapers, postcards

Selection of charms, sequins, motifs

Scraps of old fabric and ribbon

Equipment
Glue brush

Scissors

Glue gun

What to do

1 Fold the white card in half – you may have to change the size of the card depending on the size of the postcard you are embellishing. Glue the postcard on the card.

2 Cut out the paper collage shapes and decide where you want to place them on the postcard. Glue them in place.

3 Cut out a piece of patterned vintage fabric and glue it to the card with PVA glue.

4 Glue the charms on the card with a hot glue gun.

5 Cut a length of ribbon or fabric and glue it along the base of the postcard with PVA glue.

lace heart

Stamping and stencilling your own designs onto paper, card and even ribbon is very satisfying and produces a card that is unique to you.

Materials

1 A5 sheet of pink card

1 A4 sheet of thin white card

1 sheet of red card (10 x 10 cm/ 4 x 4 in)

1 piece of lace (10 x 10 cm/4 x 4 in)

Pink spray paint

36-cm (15-in) length of cotton ribbon tape

Spot shape rubber stamp

Rubber stamp ink pads in pink and deep pink

Adhesive foam pads

Spray adhesive

Equipment

Scissors

Pencil

Ruler

Glue gun

Template   Page 125

What to do

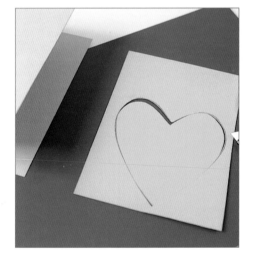

1 Fold the pink card in half. Trace or photocopy the heart template onto thin card and cut out.

2 Spray adhesive on the reverse of the piece of lace and smooth down on the red card. Spray pink paint through the lace. Allow to dry for 5 minutes and remove the lace.

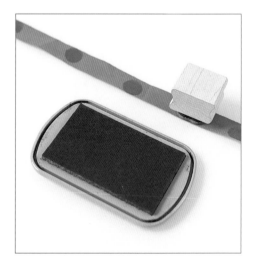

3 Stamp spots onto one side of the cotton tape ribbon with a deep pink ink.

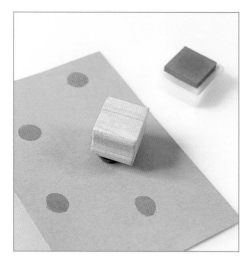

4 Stamp pink spots all over the background card, front and back.

5 Trace around the heart template on the stencilled red card and cut out the heart shape.

6 Tie the ribbon in a bow and it glue onto the heart.

7 Stick the heart on the spotty card using adhesive foam pads to raise the heart away from the design and give a 3-D effect.

button flower

This fun flower brings to life all those wasted scraps of fabric that might otherwise have been thrown away.

Materials

1 sheet of white card (18 x 12.5 cm/ 7 x 5 in)

1 A4 sheet of thin cream card

Scraps of fabric (approximately 10 different patterns)

PVA glue

Button

Equipment

Scissors

Pencil

Glue brush

Green coloured pencil

Glue gun

Templates   Page 125

What to do

1 Fold the white card in half. Photocopy or trace the petal and leaf templates onto the thin card and cut them out.

2 Draw around the templates on the reverse of the fabrics and cut out 10 petals and 2 leaves.

3 Paint a 2-cm (¾-in) diameter circle of glue, 6 cm (2¼ in) from the top of the card. Attach the inside tips of the petals on the glue and gradually work around the circle so the petals overlap each other.

4 Glue the leaves at the bottom and draw a green pencil line approximately 9 cm (3½ in) long between the flower and the leaves.

 Glue the button in the centre of the flower with a hot glue gun.

thank you chocolates

These might not be the real thing but they still look good enough to eat! This is a simple but effective card that requires a little preplanning to copy the image on to acetate.

Materials

Photograph of chocolates, or image cut from a magazine

1 A4 sheet of acetate

1 A4 sheet of pink card

1 sheet of tracing paper

1 A4 sheet of thin card

1 sheet of white paper (15 x 10.5 cm/6 x 4¼ in)

Masking tape

Double-sided tape

Spray adhesive

Equipment

Scissors

Pencil

Craft knife

Cutting mat

What to do

1 Take a picture or photograph of chocolates to a colour copier shop and ask them to copy the image onto a piece of acetate.

2 Trace the chocolate box picture on to tracing paper.

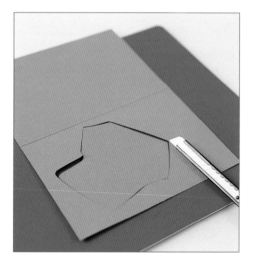

3 Cut the A4 sheet of pink card in half, then fold it in half. Transfer the chocolate box shape onto the inside of the front of the card, then cut out.

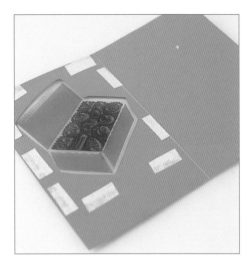

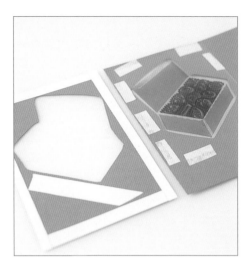

4 Cut the remaining piece of pink card in half and place one piece behind the front of the card. Draw around the chocolate box shape, then cut out the shape. The resulting stencil will be used later to finish the card.

5 Trim and stick the acetate on the inside of the front of the card with masking tape.

6 Attach the pink card stencil shape over the acetate with double-sided tape to conceal the masking tape.

7 Stick the white paper on the inside, right-hand page of the card with spray adhesive. This will enhance the colours in the acetate when the card is standing up.

gallery of everyday cards

▶**Flower garden** Here different materials and techniques complement each other. A black and white image printed onto transparent plastic is accompanied by some cut-out watercolour flowers.
Rosie Marshall

▼**Fancy footwear** A great idea that could be adapted for other objects: cut a shoe shape out of cardboard and cover one side with spotty fabric. A length of cord and a leopard-print bow complete the shoe.
Petra Boase

▶**Petal pocket** Circles of coloured card are decorated with glitter and sit together in a transparent pocket on the front of this card. Why not try a similar design with different shapes? Stars or hearts would work well.
Ilium for Pearl and Black

▲**Gold leaf** Another example of a card that has the design printed directly onto it. This time a delicate gold pattern of branches and leaves stretches across the card. Flowers or fruit shapes would be ideal for this type of design.
Kim Robertson

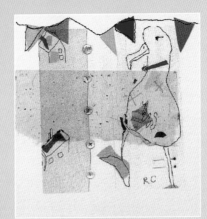

▶Stepping out A medley of materials and cleverly combined elements of collage and embroidery enhance this card with a printed background as its starting point.
Rachel Coleman

▼Ships in the night This collage uses different shades of thin blue paper to represent the sea. The lighthouse is made from a piece of wood and some pink textured fabric.
Big Sky Designs

▲Island hopping Felt has been used to make the island, sun, palm tree and girl. Some details have been drawn by hand and wobbly eyes bring it to life.
Jennifer Montgomery for Pearl and Black

▲▲A stitch in time The clothes-line is picked out in embroidery while fine paper glued over part of the card gives the design more depth.
Rachel Coleman

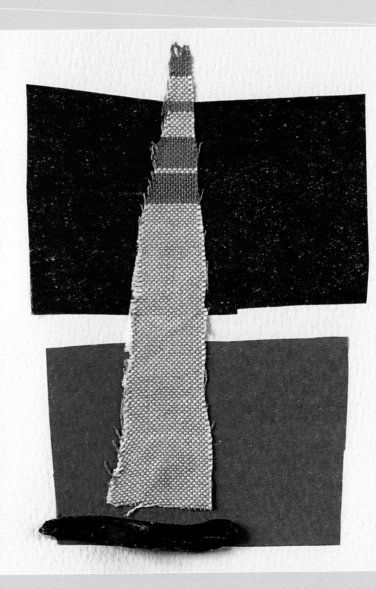

◄The bee's knees Yellow and black stripy fur fabric is glued onto both sides of the card and a pair of wobbly eyes turns it into a bumble bee, or maybe a tiger! Look out for different fur materials to create other animals.
The Monster Factory

►Pretty impressive
This card has patterned paper in the centre, which is overlaid with a tiny paper bird and foam shapes, customized with little glass beads and a pink jewel.
Rosie Marshall

▲Bright and breezy An abstract blue design has been laser-printed onto bright yellow card for a summery feel. If you have a creative hand, try painting your own designs directly onto cards.
Kim Robertson

▲Soft as velvet This elegant devouré design has a lovely velvety sheen complimented by the intricate detail of the leaves.
Kim Robertson

▲Floral display Metallic card has been cut into shapes to make a basket and little paper flowers have been arranged at the top. You can buy these flowers and other shapes, ready-made in craft shops.
Aurelia for Pearl and Black

▼Flight of fancy This design uses fine embroidery to create a beautiful pink butterfly. Different fabrics are stitched together and tiny dabs of glitter catch the light.
Vicky King

▲Colour craze Here, the different elements of the design have been worked together and then laser copied. This gives the appearance of collage. A single star glitters in the centre.
Rosie Marshall

▲A stitch-up Different fabrics have been carefully stitched on top of one another and extra detail is added to create a pretty flower. Glitter and a button add the final touches.
Vicky King

All the patterns, motifs and designs required for the card projects are included in the following pages. They are reproduced in this book at one hundred per cent, so you simply need to trace them off using tracing paper and a pencil, or photocopy them onto paper and transfer the design to card if required. If you wish to enlarge or reduce a template pattern, you can do this on a photocopier by keying in the required percentage before copying.

Templa

tes

bobbing snowmen
(see pages 18–19)

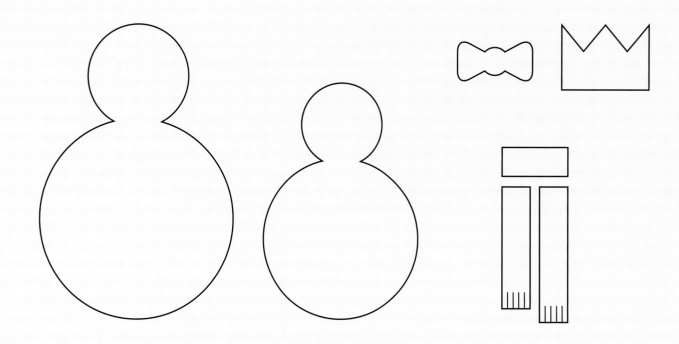

spinning star
(see pages 20–21)

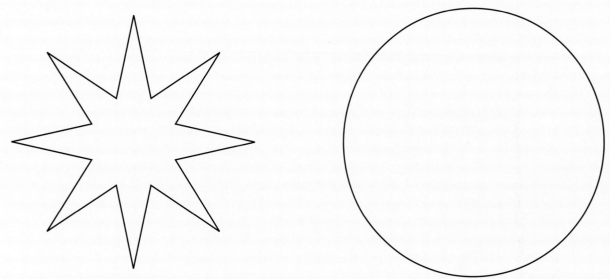

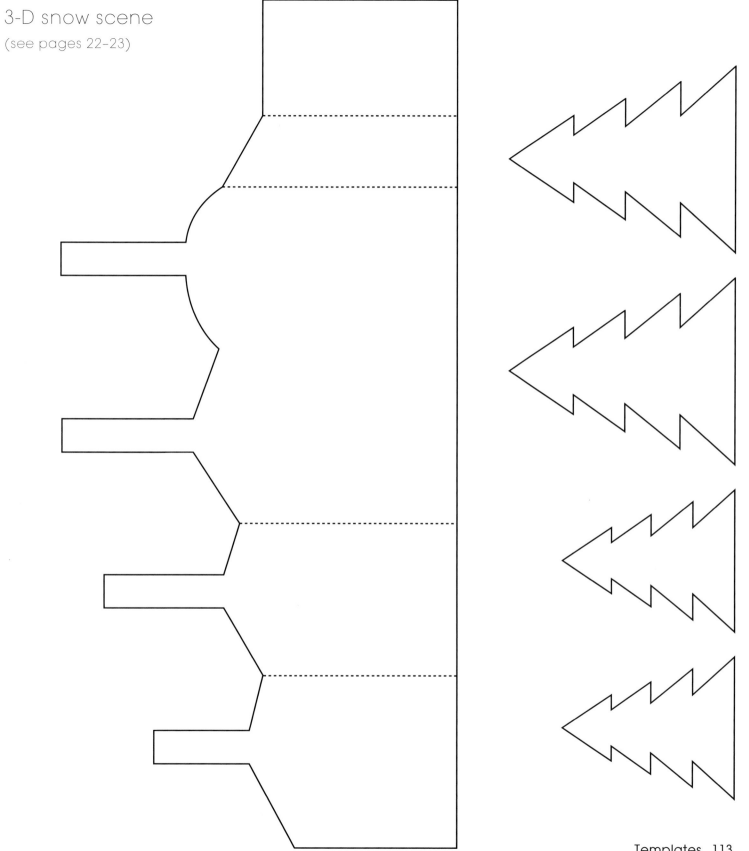

3-D snow scene
(see pages 22–23)

Templates 113

golden reindeer

(see pages 24–25)

christmas cracker

(see pages 26–27)

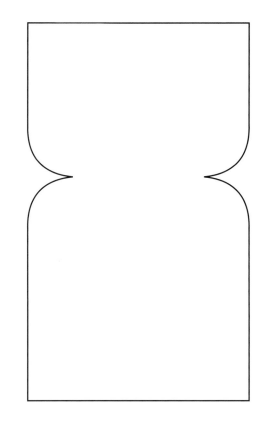

silk painted eggs

(see pages 28–29)

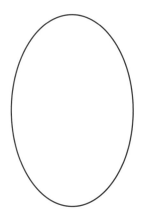

pom-pom bunny
(see pages 30–31)

thanksgiving, shaker-style
(see pages 32–33)

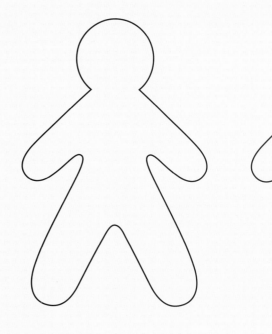

wedding cake
(see pages 40–41)

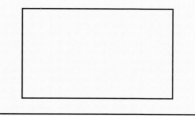

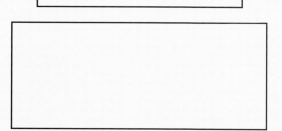

confetti church

(see pages 42–43)

diamond ring

(see pages 44–45)

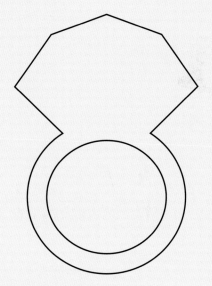

baby bootee

(see pages 46–47)

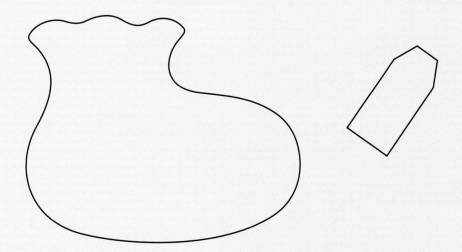

new home

(see pages 50–51)

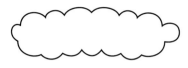

needlepoint house

(see pages 52–53)

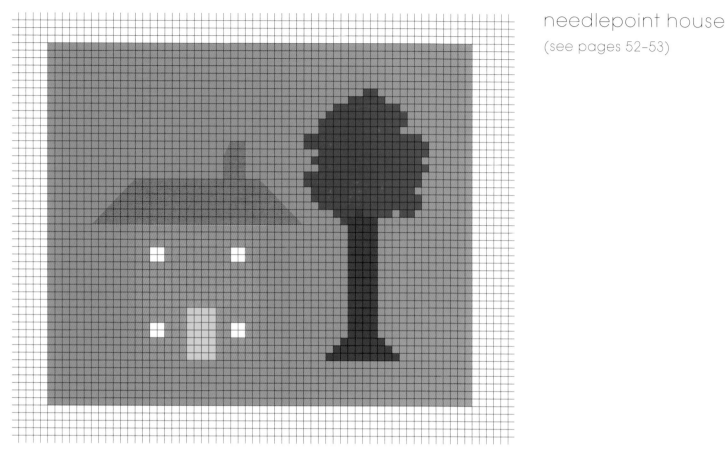

mother's day wire flowers

(see pages 54–55)

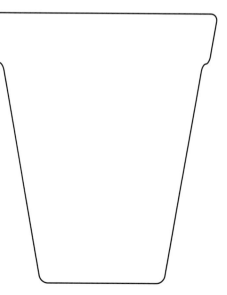

father's day photo card
(see pages 56–57)

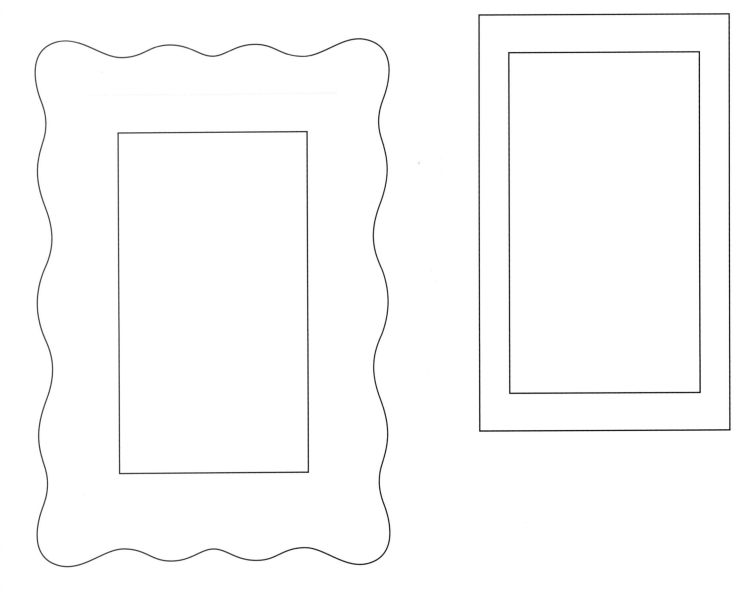

embossed tin love heart
(see pages 58–59)

champagne congratulations
(see pages 60–61)

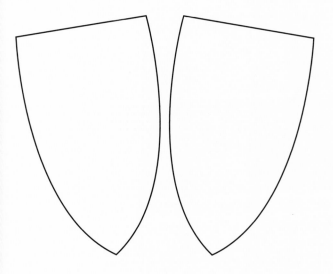

good luck horseshoe
(see pages 62–63)

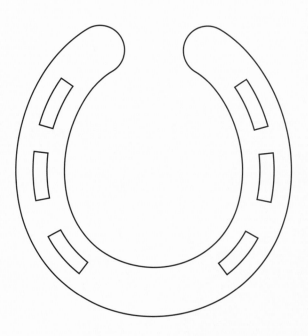

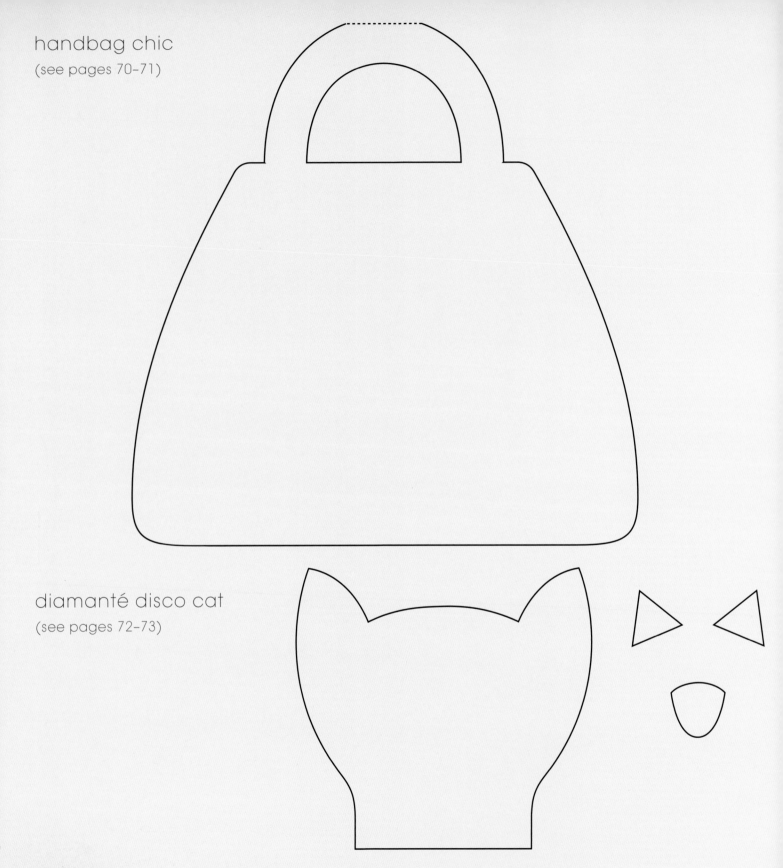

handbag chic
(see pages 70–71)

diamanté disco cat
(see pages 72–73)

embroidered cup cake

(see pages 74-75)

stained glass flowers
(see pages 80–81)

party girl
(see pages 84–85)

photo fun rosette
(see pages 82–83)

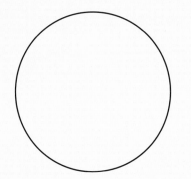

stripey paper fruit
(see pages 92–93)

bon voyage
(see pages 94–95)

butterfly surprise
(see pages 96–97)

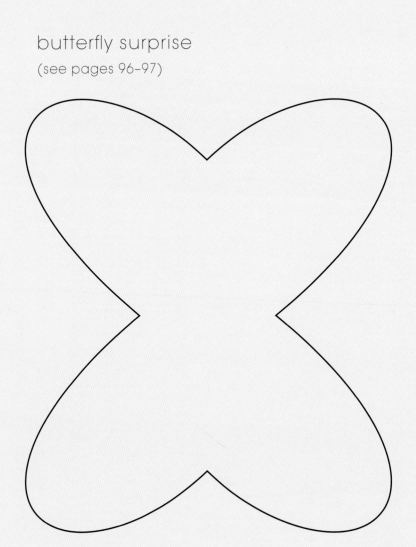

lace heart

(see pages 100–101)

button flower

(see pages 102–103)

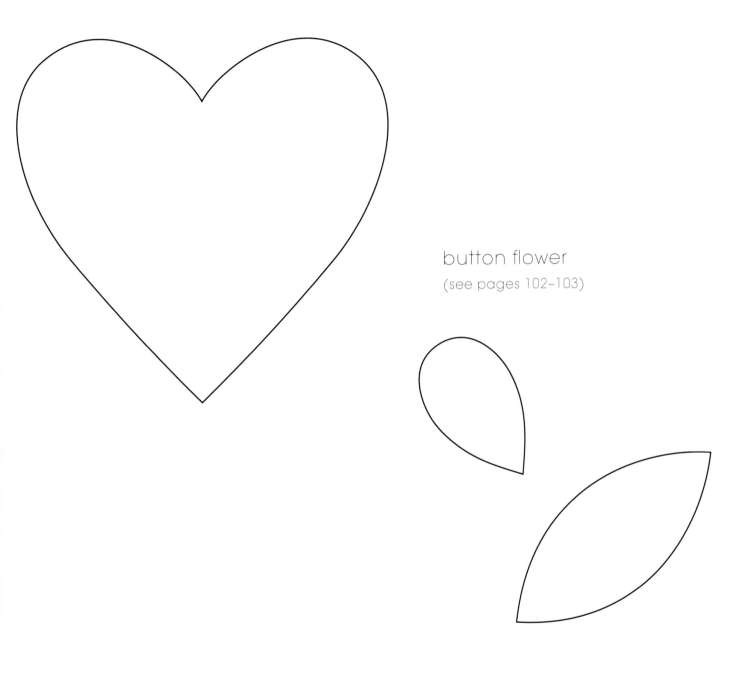

Index

A
Acorn Art 67, 89
address labels 15
adhesives 10
Air Mail 89
All That Glitters 65
Animal Magic 34
anniversary cards 32, 58–61
  All That Glitters 65
  Champagne
    Congratulations 60–1, 119
  Elegant Embroidery 65
  Embossed Tin Love Heart 6,
    38, 58–9, 119
  Jewel of a Card 65
  Simply Stunning 65
appliqué 6
  stitches 14
art and craft stores 7

B
babies see new baby cards
Baby Bootee 46–7, 116
Baby Patchwork 7, 48–9
Bee in your Bonnet 86
Bees Knees 108
Big Sky Designs 66, 107
birthday cards 6, 68–89
  Air Mail 89
  Bee in your Bonnet 86
  Birthday 88
  Birthday Countdown 86
  Cut the Cake 86
  Diamanté Disco Cat 72–3,
    120
  Dreamscape 88
  Dressing Up 89
  Embroidered Cupcake 7,
    74–5, 121
  gallery of 86–9
  Handbag Chic 70–1, 120
  It's a Gift 86
  Naturally Elegant 89
  New Look 88
  Oriental Pressed Flowers
    76–7

Party Girl 84–5, 122
Pass the Parcel 89
Perfect Print 87
Pet Project 88
Photo Fun Rosette 82–3, 123
Polka Dot Present 7, 78–9
Say it with Flowers 87
Spot the Difference 87
Stained Glass Flowers 80–1,
  122
templates 120–2
Velvet Crush 87
Birthday Countdown 86
blanket stitch 14
Boase, Petra 37, 66, 67, 87, 88
Bobbing Snowmen 18–19, 112
Bon Voyage 6, 14, 94–5, 124
Branching Out 34
Bright and Breezy 108
Butterfly Surprise 96–7, 124
Button Flower 7, 90, 102–3, 125

C
Champagne Congratulations
  60–1, 119
Charming Card 66
Christening cards 48
Christmas cards 6, 16, 18–27,
  34–5
  3 D Snow Scene 22–3, 113
  Animal Magic 34
  Bobbing Snowmen 18–19,
    112
  Branching Out 34
  Christmas Cracker 26–7, 114
  Christmas Stocking 35
  Fairy Dust 35
  Golden Reindeer 13, 24–5,
    114
  Pretty in Pink 34
  Sew Special 35
  Snow Storm 35
  Spinning Star 20–1, 112
  Starry, Starry Night 34
  templates 112–14
Classic Kitsch 37

clay modelling 50–1
Coleman, Rachel 36, 107
collage 6, 16
Colour Craze 109
Confetti Church 42–3, 116
Cut the Cake 86
cutting out equipment 8

D
decorations 10–11
decoupage 6
Diamanté Disco Cat 72–3, 120
Diamond Ring 44–5, 116
Dreamscape 88
Dressing Up 89

E
Easter cards 6, 28–31, 36
  Easter Cross 36
  Funny Bunny 36
  Groovy Chick 36
  Metallic Egg 36
  Pom Pom Bunny 30–1, 115
  Silk Painted Eggs 28–9
  templates 115
Elegant Embroidery 65
Embossed Tin Love Heart 6, 38,
  58–9, 119
Embroidered Cupcake 7, 74–5,
  121
engagement card, Diamond
  Ring 44–5, 116
envelopes 15
everyday greetings 6, 90–109
  gallery 106–9
  templates 123–5
everyday items, decorating
  cards with 7

F
fabrics 11
Fairy Dust 35
Fancy Footwear 106
Father's Day photo card 38,
  56–7, 118
Ferrier, Kathleen 36

festive fun 6, 16–37
Flight of Fancy 109
Floral Display 109
Flower Garden 106
Flower Power 37
folding cards 13
Funny Bunny 36

G
galleries
  birthday cards 86–9
  celebration cards 64–7
  everyday cards 106–9
  festive cards 34–7
Gardner, Caroline 34, 65, 66
Glitterati 37
gold leaf, applying 13
Gold Leaf card 106
Golden Reindeer 13, 24–5,
  114
Good Luck Horseshoe 6, 14,
  62–3, 119
Groovy Chick 36

H
Hall, Camilla 37
Handbag Chic 70–1, 120
Hanging by a Thread 67
Heester, Kate 37
Hewlings, Maud 88
Horseshoe, Good Luck 6, 14,
  62–3, 119
House of Cards 66
houses see new home cards

I
inks 11
invitations 6
Island Hopping 107
It's a Boy 67
It's a Gift 86

J
Jewel of a Card 65
jewellery pliers 8, 9
Jones, Leigh 36

Acknowledgements

Gallery spreads – contributors

Rosie Marshall
e. rosiemarshall@blueyonder.co.uk
www.rosiemarshall.co.uk

Rachel Coleman
t. 01695 575586
www.rachelcolemandesigns.co.uk

Kim Robertson
t. 020 7242 6103
e. kimrobertsonw8@hotmail.com

The Monster Factory
t. 020 8875 9988/020 8870 4488
e. www.themonsterfactory.com

Vicky King
t. 01803 866700/782050
e. vickyking@btinternet.com

Abigail Mill
t. 01603 452 513
e. abigail@abigailmill.co.uk
www.abigailmill.co.uk

Maud Hewlings
t. 07779 018950

G.F. Smith & Son
(supplied paper and envelopes for the photoshoot)
t. 01482 323503

Caroline Gardner
t. 020 8288 9696
info@carolinegardner.com
www.carolinegardner.com

Aurelia for Pearl & Black
t. 020 77586 5868

Jennifer Montgomery for Pearl & Black
t. 020 7586 5868

Jennifer Montgomery for Funky Eclectica
t. 01484 385656

Ilium at Pearl & Black
t. 020 7586 5868

Pearl & Black
t. 020 7586 5868

Nosey Parker Cards for Pearl & Black
t. 020 7586 5868

Katie Heester
www.katieheester.co.uk

Camilla Hall/White Space designs
t. 0117 902 5865
e. info@whitespacedesigns.co.uk

Kathryn Ferrier
t. 01884 840440

Big Sky Design
t. 01263 740266

Executive Editor Sarah Tomley
Senior Editor Rachel Lawrence
Executive Art Director Leigh Jones
Designer Miranda Harvey
Photography Peter Pugh-Cook © Octopus Publishing Group Limited
Senior Production Controller Manjit Sihra